THE DOG WHO RESCUES CATS

THE DOG WHO RESCUES CATS

THE TRUE STORY OF GINNY

PHILIP GONZALEZ AND LEONORE FLEISCHER

INTRODUCTION BY CLEVELAND AMORY

SIMON & SCHUSTER
A VIACOM COMPANY

First published in Great Britain by Simon & Schuster Ltd, 1997
A Viacom company

Published by arrangement with HarperCollins Publishers, Inc.,
New York, New York USA

Simon & Schuster Ltd
West Garden Place
Kendal Street
London W2 2AQ

Simon & Schuster Australia
Sydney

A CIP catalogue record for this book is available from the British Library

ISBN 0-684-81924-4

Printed and bound in Great Britain by
Butler & Tanner Ltd, Frome and London

To Ginny and to Vogue.

—PHILIP GONZALEZ

To my son Alexander, to my grandson Theodore, and to my cat Mitzi.

—LEONORE FLEISCHER

ACKNOWLEDGMENTS

Phyllis Levy, who started it all by publishing an article about Ginny and me in *Good Housekeeping*.

Freya Manston, who knew our story should be a book and made it happen.

Cleveland Amory, one of Ginny's first believers, a giant in animal rescue whose books have been an inspiration to me.

My editor, Larry Ashmead, for all his enthusiasm.

Jed Mattes, for his kind support.

Ginny's "Mommy," Sheilah, who was in on all of it from the beginning.

With special thanks to my veterinarians, Lewis Gelfand, D.V.M., and Andrea Kuperschmid, D.V.M., who have made it possible for Ginny and me to help so many cats.

With special thanks, too, to Ken Colon, Ginny's first friend and protector.

And to all of Ginny's other friends.

Contents

INTRODUCTION

NOT SINCE THE APPEARANCE of the late Paul Gallico's immortal classic, *The Snow Goose*, has there been such a touching saga of animal rescue as *The Dog Who Rescues Cats*. Gallico's book was about a disabled man who lives near the shore and rescues first snow geese from hunters, and then, at Dunkirk, British soldiers from Germans.

The Dog Who Rescues Cats is also the story of a disabled man who lives near the shore and rescues. But here the similarity between the two books ends. While the man rescues first a dog and then a long succession of cats, he does not really do these rescues himself—his dog does them. And cats, supposedly the archenemies of dogs, become, in this book, the dog's archfriends. Furthermore, they do so with hardly a hint of archness about it.

The man's name is Philip Gonzalez. He is a Vietnam veteran who, while not injured in the war, was afterward so injured in an industrial accident that, among other problems, he lost the use of his right arm.

Although Philip is the author, with Leonore Fleischer, of *The Dog Who Rescues Cats*, he modestly relegates himself to a secondary role in his book. The true hero of the book is the dog. Her name is Ginny. She is very definitely an indefinite mixed breed—one part schnauzer, one part husky, and one part anyone's guess. But there is one thing of which Ginny is all part, and that is heart. From start to finish she is not only the initiator of almost every rescue she and her master make, she is also the one who ensures that each and every one of them end, as they should end, happily.

Night after night, starting out late (or early in the morning, depending on which way you look at it), Philip and Ginny begin their rounds about 4:30 A.M., because that is apparently the best time to rescue cats. Together the two of them patrol—Ginny on a leash, Philip holding the leash— their by-no-means-affluent neighborhood. They examine every possible location in which a cat would find refuge—in dark alleys, in abandoned buildings, in empty lots, in junkyards, and even right on the street. And over and over what Ginny usually rescues is a cat who is disabled. The very first cat Ginny ever rescued was deaf, the second was missing an eye. Another early rescue was of a cat without any hind feet. Still another was so brain-damaged she could do nothing but roll where she wanted to go.

Every single one of these cats finds, in the Gonzalez home, his or her home. And something you will find, too, as you read this book, is that over and over you will have to pinch yourself to realize that what you are reading is not fiction—it is fact. Every one of these incredible rescues really did take place. I know this myself because I was fortunate enough to meet Philip and Ginny personally, and also meet and play with their now vast feline assembly. I have never forgotten a single one of them. I have certainly not forgotten Betty Boop, who has no back feet, or Topsy, who cannot do anything but roll to get anywhere.

I am equally sure that after reading this book you will never forget a single one of them, either. Especially not that very special dog named Ginny.

Cleveland Amory, author of

The Cat Who Came for Christmas

March 1995

=1=
PHILIP

THIS IS THE TRUE STORY of the most amazing dog I've ever known. Yes, I admit I'm prejudiced because I love her so much, but I'm not alone in making this claim. Just about everybody who has ever met her says she's unique; they always tell me that they've never even heard of a pup like her. This dog has been written about and talked about by many people; part of her inspirational story was even published as an article in *Good Housekeeping* magazine, but there is still a lot left to tell. This little dog has changed a lot of lives, human as well as animal lives. Beginning with mine. Especially mine.

This is the true story of my dog. Her name is Ginny.

My name is Philip Gonzalez. I was born forty-five years ago in Mayaguez, Puerto Rico, but I was brought to New York when I was only seven months old, and I never went back. All my life has been lived near the Atlantic Ocean, first in Far Rockaway and now in another beach community in Long Island. We were a large family of children. First came the three boys, of whom I was the youngest. Jose, Peter, then me, then my three sisters, Nancy and the twins, Maria and Marguerita.

We were a close family, even though there was thirteen years' difference in ages between the oldest, Jose, and the youngest, the twins. We did a lot of things together as a family. Because we lived near the ocean, we spent a lot of time at the beach all summer, but we also went to street fairs and carnivals, watched the fireworks together on the Fourth of July, and planned picnics and cookouts. Since all six of us brothers and sisters had a lot of friends, our apartment was usually overflowing with kids of all ages.

I would definitely call my childhood a happy one. I was an active boy, and loved sports, especially the ball games the neighborhood boys played in the streets—stickball and handball—but I also played racquetball and paddleball on courts. I was too small and lightweight for football, but I always enjoyed watching it.

When I was nineteen, I went into the service, joining the U.S. Army. I served in Vietnam, and yes, I saw combat, but I don't like to talk about it. It was a dark episode in my life, one that I would much rather not remember. Also, my mother died in 1971, while I was in 'Nam, and one of my brothers died suddenly the year before, so that was another reason to try to forget that sorrowful time.

How I came to ship out to 'Nam is a strange chapter in my life. Because I volunteered for the service without waiting to be drafted, I had my choice of serving in Vietnam or Germany. I didn't have a death wish, so naturally I opted for Germany.

I did my basic training at Fort Dix in New Jersey and had started on AIT, Advanced Individual Training. My brother Peter came to see me the day before my regiment was to go out on bivouac. It was visitors' day at the camp, and Peter brought along Jose's little daughter, Cindy, our niece. We had a good time together, but Peter appeared to be upset at the thought that I might be ordered to 'Nam.

"No way, man," I assured him, "I'm going to Germany. Guaranteed."

Peter shook his head. "I don't like it. If they send you to 'Nam, I'm gonna tell them to take me instead."

I was touched at Peter's concern and his affection. The two of us were closer together in age than I was with any of my other siblings, so there was an especially strong bond between us. Peter was my closest friend in the world, and it made me feel good to think he felt the same way about me.

The next day we went out on bivouac, sleeping in tents in the woods and eating field rations. That night I was walking through the woods to my tent, when I stumbled over something. It was a freshly dug grave. Not a real grave, of course, but a hole in the ground some of the guys had dug for a gag. They'd erected a make-believe headstone on it that read REST IN PEACE, G.I. JOE. Even though I recognized it for a joke, the "grave" made me uneasy.

When I got to my tent, something dark and large leaped out at me, scaring me half to death. It was a toad, a really huge one. It shouldn't have startled me, because there's nothing uncommon about a toad in the woods, but remember, I was a city boy who'd never seen one up close.

As I tried to go to sleep that night, I could hear thunder and see lightning for hours. The whole night struck me as pretty creepy—first the grave, then the toad, and afterward, the storm. Like a Halloween night. I didn't close my eyes until very late, and I slept for only a few hours.

When I woke up the next morning, a lieutenant was walking down the line of tents, yelling, "Peter Gonzalez! Who's Peter Gonzalez? Is there a Peter Gonzalez here?"

"My name is Philip Gonzalez," I called out. "And I have a brother named Peter."

"Then it's gotta be you. Your brother died last night." Just like that. No warning, no preamble, no sympathy.

I went into shock. Peter? Dead? How was this possible? "H-how? Wh-what happened?" I could only stammer.

"Automobile accident. Better get back to the base. You're going home for the funeral."

I handed over my rifle and climbed into a jeep, back to Fort Dix. I changed into my class A's, my best uniform, and headed for Far Rockaway on the bus. I didn't stop to call home, because if I had, I would have missed the next bus. As it was, I made it only by a whisker. I was so numb I wasn't even thinking. I'd seen Peter only yesterday, alive and well, and now he was dead! It didn't make sense. What if he'd died on the way home from the army base? I'd feel guilty about that all my life. Had there been an auto accident? And what about little Cindy? Had she been injured? All the way home, those questions preyed on my mind.

When I got home I discovered that Peter had not died in

an accident. He'd passed away with a sudden heart attack, although he was very young. It was a sad day for the Gonzalez family when we buried Peter. And my mother didn't outlive him for long. She died the following year.

When I returned to Fort Dix, I volunteered for Vietnam. I can't explain why; it was just something I felt I had to do. Probably I had lost interest in my own life; maybe I'd even developed that death wish I hadn't had earlier. But I know that I felt guilty about being alive when Peter was dead.

But the strangeness didn't end there. At Thanksgiving, they shipped us out, destination Vietnam. Not on a ship, but on a military transport plane. They call them Military Airlift Command, or MAC, flights. On the way to 'Nam, we made a landing at Anchorage, to refuel and to pick up four more passengers. The MAC flight was completely filled, and the four new guys outranked us, so three of my buddies and I were bumped and left behind on the ground to wait for the next transport. We were wearing jungle fatigues, and it gets pretty damn cold in Anchorage in November, so as you can imagine we weren't too happy about the bumping, and we grumbled and complained about it between chattering teeth.

Our plane took off without us, and as we stood on the tarmac watching it go, the aircraft made a sudden veer and headed straight for the earth, where it crashed. A fireball erupted, and between the crash and the flames every life on board was lost. By a quirk of fate, just one of those things, the only men spared were the four of us left behind on the ground.

The army hustled us onto a plane and flew us to

Elmendorph Air Force Base without even letting us call home to tell our folks we were alive. The authorities decided to contain the tragic story until they could release the news in the most efficient and least traumatic way for the next of kin. It wasn't until we landed in Japan that I was allowed to send my mother a postcard, saying, "I'm alive. I wasn't on the plane that crashed." Not even a phone call; they only authorized a postcard. Up until the moment she received my card, my mother believed I was dead, and I'm sure that the shock of that, combined with my brother Peter's recent death, helped to kill her.

One thing, though, came out of that terrible experience. I stopped being afraid of going into combat. I figured that if God had wanted to take me, he'd had plenty of opportunities already and he'd passed them up. So maybe he was saving me for something. What I never suspected was the strange destiny he was saving me for.

MY EARLY LIFE WITH DOGS AND CATS

My experience with animals wasn't very wide or deep, but it started early. I was nine years old, walking down the street one day, when an older boy I knew slightly from the neighborhood stopped me and said, "Here, you want this?"

He put something warm and furry into my hand, and when I looked down, it was the tiniest kitten I had ever seen in my life, not much more than newborn. I took her home, but nobody except me believed that she would survive. I fed that kitten with milk in an eyedropper night and day, and she surprised us all by growing up. I named her Sylvia, and for years I fed her and changed her litter, but to tell the truth, she was the family cat, never particularly mine.

My sister was allergic to cats, so we had to keep Sylvia in a separate part of the apartment. She turned into an attack cat, and she was ready to rip everybody apart except for family members. People were actually afraid to come in through the front door. Sylvia seemed to like us well enough; she never scratched a Gonzalez. The funny thing about her was that, ferocious as she was, she never ate meat or fish. Cats are carnivorous animals, but—maybe because I hand-raised her on milk—Sylvia's chosen diet was only milk and bread. She wouldn't touch cat food or even chicken or beef from our table. One year there was a milk strike in New York, and in order to keep Sylvia fed, my mother had to walk for many blocks to find a quart of milk, and she had to pay fifty cents for it, instead of a quarter, its usual price.

Sylvia lived for eight years, never growing any fonder of meat or fish or strangers. She was the first and last cat that ever saw the inside of the Gonzalez household. Later in life, while I was living with a girlfriend, she adopted two cats from the Bide-A-Wee animal shelter. When we broke up and she moved out, the cats, Sophie and Sheba, stayed behind. Maybe they liked me better, or maybe they just liked the apartment, but they didn't want to move. I kept them for a while, but when I heard of a family who needed a couple of pets for their boy who was confined to bed, I let the cats go to a new home, and they made him very happy. It never occurred to me to replace them with other cats.

Frankly, cats were never great favorites of mine. I guess I

believed all those stupid stories people make up about them—that cats are aloof, disloyal, not affectionate, even "sneaky," although I'm not sure what people mean when they say that. I think it has something to do with the fact that cats can retract their front claws and dogs can't. So a cat can cross a room almost silently, but a dog's claws will go *click click* on the bare wood, as though the dog is up-front about where he's going, but the cat deliberately tries to disguise her movements. People can be really dumb about things they don't understand. Ignorance often leads to fear and hate, as I was to find out later in life.

But if I was indifferent to cats, I did like dogs. When I was eighteen years old, we sort of got a dog. Husky's owner worked in the same place as my brother Peter, and when the man died, his family was ready to put the dog to sleep. He wasn't a young dog—maybe seven or eight years old—but he was still in good shape and had a gusto for life, and it would have been a shame to put him down. Husky was a purebred collie about twice the size of Lassie. The landlord wouldn't let us keep a dog in our apartment, so my brother and I "smuggled" Husky in and out, hiding him during the day (which wasn't easy, considering his size) and walking him only at night. Lucky for us (and for him) Husky almost never barked; he was a sweet, friendly, outgoing dog who expressed himself by wagging his tail furiously whenever anybody talked to him.

I had lived with Husky only about two years when I joined the army.

Poor Husky came to a very sad end. My oldest brother, Jose, had left home and was living on his own, and he had a German shepherd named Vicky, a really nice, friendly pup.

Husky went to visit them often, and he and Vicky played together like pals. One day the two dogs were in Jose's fenced yard. As it happened, they were both tied, but evidently a couple of large dogs were roaming loose in the neighborhood, barking and showing their teeth, frightening women and children. Complaints had been made to the police.

An officer came to Jose's house and accused Vicky and Husky of terrorizing the neighbors. Jose protested that the dogs had not been roaming loose, that they'd been tied up in the backyard all afternoon and couldn't possibly be guilty, and besides, these were not vicious animals, but friendly dogs who liked people.

But the police officer wouldn't listen. He'd been looking for two dogs, and now he'd found two dogs. That's all he needed to know. Before Jose could say or do anything to stop him, the cop drew his revolver from its holster and shot both dogs dead. Two innocent lives snuffed out in seconds.

When I read about it in a letter from home I went into shock. It was totally beyond me. I couldn't imagine anybody being so cruel to helpless animals. I only wish I could say that this was the last instance of such human cruelty I ever encountered. But of course it wasn't.

In 'Nam, one of the guys in our outfit wanted to shoot a water buffalo. There are a lot of water buffalo in Vietnam; the villagers use them for farming and they are important to a family's survival and a village's economy. He was taking aim when I stopped him.

"Leave the thing alone," I said. "You want to shoot something, shoot a V.C. coming at you with a weapon. That animal has no weapon, so don't shoot it."

I myself was very good with a rifle. I qualified as Sharpshooter and then Expert, which was better. Out of 120 targets I hit 118. But when I got out of the service and the guys on my job site wanted me to go hunting with them, I wouldn't. I never saw any reason to kill another living creature, and I always despised cruelty of any kind.

MONTOOSE

After I came back from Vietnam and got out of the service, I got myself a dog of my own, a small mixed breed I called Montoose. It wasn't my original intention to get or keep a dog. I was just taking a walk on the beach when I saw two little boys heading for the water, and one of them had a tiny puppy in his hands.

"Where are you going with that pup?" I asked.

"Our mom says we can't keep it, so we're going to throw it into the water and drown it," one of the boys answered.

Even though I didn't particularly want a dog I couldn't stand the thought of murdering that little fellow. "No, give me the pup. I'll take care of it."

I carried the puppy home from the beach wrapped in my shirt; he couldn't have been more than five or six weeks old, much too young to be without a mother. I was going to have to be his mother, at least until I could find a good home for him. He must have thought I *was* his mother, because he took to trotting after me everywhere I went, just like a little shadow.

He was a Dobie-collie mix, black and brown like a

Doberman, but with the pointed face of a collie. He was really cute, and I fed him several times a day, first milk, and later meat and chicken, and then finally dog food. The dog ate with a voracious appetite, growing bigger and stronger every day. At last he was old enough to go to a new home.

A friend of mine had told me he'd take him off my hands, so he came to the house to get the pup. I had every intention of letting the dog go, but when I looked down at him (he was sitting on the floor, as close to me as he could get, as usual), I just didn't have the heart.

"Sorry, but I changed my mind. I'm keeping him," I told my friend. "I'm going to call him Montoose."

Montoose was the name of one of my army buddies, and I always thought that would make a good name for a dog. He was a great little pup, as smart and friendly as they come. He didn't grow very big, only about thirty pounds. We became tight buddies, and I would walk him at 5:30 in the morning, before going off to work. Montoose loved his walks, and he used to wake me every morning, at about 5:15, as reliable as an alarm clock.

One morning Montoose woke me up at 4:15, an hour too early. He had his leash in his mouth, as he always did.

"No, Montoose, go away. Let me sleep. I still got an hour to sleep," I begged him.

But Montoose wouldn't leave. He put his paws on my bed and scratched at the covers, whining and yipping. He didn't let up. At last I was beaten. I dragged myself out of bed, pulled my jeans on, put on my shoes, and grabbed my overcoat. If Montoose wanted to go walking at 4:30 A.M., who was I to say no?

As soon as we hit the street, Montoose began acting very strangely. He started to tug at his leash, really hard, dragging me off in a direction we had never taken. I just followed his lead. As we came close to a Baptist church in my neighborhood, Montoose began to bark and wouldn't quit. He kept dragging me in the direction of the church, barking and yipping at the top of his lungs.

Suddenly I smelled smoke. I looked toward the church and could see red flames begin to flicker behind the tall windows. The Baptist church was on fire!

I ran toward the nearest fire call box, but it had been vandalized and was broken. So Montoose and I headed for home on the double, and I called the fire department on my home phone. The fire engines got there in short order, and they managed to save most of the church.

The next day the fire department telephoned me and asked me how I had known that the church was on fire. There had been a rash of church and synagogue arsons in and around Far Rockaway recently, and the authorities were looking for the arsonists. I told them about Montoose, and about how he'd nagged me to get out of bed an hour early. The firefighter told me that if no one had reported the fire for another hour, the church would surely have burned to the ground. Montoose was a hero, he said, a real hero. Of course, I agreed.

Still I kept wondering. How did Montoose know? What kind of magic had he used, or what sort of sixth sense did he have? But I kept my questions to myself, because Montoose wasn't giving me any answers.

I was working long hours and I hated to leave Montoose

all alone in my apartment, so I would take him over to my brother Jose's delicatessen and leave him there for "baby-sitting."

One day, when Montoose was only a little over two years old, he was at Jose's deli, tied outside, and sitting well up on the sidewalk right in front of the store. It was winter, and the roads and streets were icy. A Long Island Lighting Company truck took a corner much too fast. It hit a patch of ice, lost traction, mounted the sidewalk, and barreled over poor little Montoose, killing him instantly. I was devastated. After Montoose died I didn't want another dog. Burying a pet was just too heartbreaking. It was better not to get involved at all than suffer the loss of a friend like Montoose.

So my personal knowledge of pets was limited, and not all that happy. Husky had been shot; Montoose had been run over. I knew only that I didn't care all that much for cats, and I liked dogs best when they were big and of a good breed, and preferably male, like Husky.

When I got out of the service in 1972, I found work in construction as a steam fitter. I held jobs in construction for eighteen years, working for New York City on the renovation of Ellis Island, and for private corporations on the World Trade Center, Columbia-Presbyterian Hospital, and other major landmark buildings.

I enjoyed the work; to me it seemed an important job, constructing permanent pieces of New York. The work was hard and exhausting, but I liked that, too, because I was young, strong, and up to its demands. And it paid very well.

Once, I was working on a building in downtown Manhattan. My men were installing a sprinkler system, working at night because the office building was occupied by day. I was in charge of the crew. We would get our deliveries on the loading dock, and sometimes we'd sit there to eat our dinner. I noticed this rat going in and out, and it seemed to me that it was always the same rat. So one night I took a flashlight and snooped around. Sure enough, in the back of the dock, I found the rat. "It" was a "she," and she had a nest of little babies. I brought her some cheese, because I knew that all rodents love cheese. And she was no exception. But like all rats she would eat anything. I left some of my dinner every day so she would have food. I didn't go too close to the rat, or try to touch her. I would just put the food down and back off. When I turned up the next night, yesterday's food would be gone to the last crumb.

One night I went to feed the rat, but I couldn't get through. There was a large load of heavy garbage blocking its nest. The mother and children were trapped behind the mound of trash.

"Come on," I said to my crew. "We gotta move it out of the way."

"What for?" They wanted to know. "It's okay where it is."

"Because there's a mother rat and her little babies trapped behind it."

I thought the guys would explode. "You're nuts!" they all yelled at me. "Move a ton of garbage for a *rat*?!"

"It will soon be Mother's Day," I told them, but that didn't seem to cut any ice.

"It's still a rat," they grumbled, but to me it was more than a rat. She was a living creature needing help.

Even though they put up a protest, I was the crew boss,

so they moved the garbage and I got to feed my rat. Not that I wanted to make her a pet. I just wanted to lend her a hand.

I always had a great respect for life, even back when I was young and thoughtless. I even used to feed pigeons, which are so numerous in New York City they're said to be rats with wings. When we were building a new unit at Columbia-Presbyterian Hospital, I would always give the pigeons bread from my lunch. I fed them every day for six months, but they would never come close or eat from my hand. They were streetwise pigeons, paranoid about everything.

I fed the birds at Ellis Island, too. One of the men in the crew had a baby pigeon, and the guy threw the little bird up in the air to make it fly. But it wasn't old enough to fly, so the pigeon fell into the water.

"You can't leave it there, it'll drown," I told him. "Go into the water and get it out."

"I'm not getting my feet wet for a pigeon," he snarled at me. The baby pigeon was floundering around in the water, fluttering its soaked wings, desperate not to sink.

"All right, then. I'll do it." I kicked off my shoes.

That shamed the guy, and he waded in himself and brought the pigeon out safely. I always hated to see a living thing hurt, especially by a human who ought to know better.

THE ACCIDENT

It was while I was working on the UPS Building a few years ago that I had the terrible accident that nearly cost me my right arm.

I was putting some tools away and I was walking past the gang box, a big tool box, when the 300 reached out and got me. The 300 is a big machine that cuts and threads large pipe. As I was going past it, a pipe about twenty-one feet long was being cut and threaded. The pipe was revolving, and it caught on my engineer's coat, and I was trapped and dragged along by the machine.

I tried to tear the coat free with my right hand, but as luck would have it, the coat was new and stiff. Engineers' coats are made of a heavy denim like canvas, a fabric that gets softer with washing, and when they're soft you can tear them. But with a new coat the fabric doesn't give. So instead of my breaking free, the revolving pipe caught my hand and arm. I don't remember anything after that, because my head slammed into the ground and I lost consciousness. Afterward, my co-workers told me that I was spun around with the rotating pipe five times and hit my head on the concrete floor five times, while the machine was busy chewing up my right arm.

The machine operator froze when he saw what was happening and couldn't take any action. Another worker dashed across the floor and pulled the plug on the 300, but by that time it was too late for my arm.

I was rushed to St. Clare's Hospital for emergency surgery. When I woke up I was in the emergency room and a doctor was shaking his head.

"We're going to have to take off that arm," he told me. "It's completely smashed, and we can't save it."

I didn't want to hear that. All I could think of was that I just couldn't lose my arm. With only one arm my life would be over for good. I said, "Absolutely not. No amputation. Put a cast on it."

So they called for a second opinion, and a specialist agreed to try to save the arm. They treated me for concussion, and two days later, I underwent surgery for the implantation of a stainless steel rod and microsurgery to reattach as many nerves as possible. When the operation was over they told me that there were no guarantees. There was still a good possibility that they would have to amputate the arm if the implantation and microsurgery didn't take.

I was in the hospital for eleven days, but I didn't want anybody to visit me there, especially not my family. My sisters and my brother Jose and my father, who was still alive in those days, had always known me as a strong, healthy person, and I didn't want them to see me helpless, flat on my back with tubes sticking out of me. I really wanted to be left alone as much as possible, so when the guys from the job came to see me at the hospital I didn't let them stay long.

On the twelfth day, the doctors released me on full disability, with very limited use of my right arm and hand—and I'm right-handed. Also, I'd gotten some serious head injuries when my head smacked the concrete floor five times while the machine was revolving. I was taking a lot of medication, and I could barely walk. Even with the medication, my head ached badly most of the time. All in all, I was only a shadow of the Philip Gonzalez who used to be so energetic and vital. For me, life seemed to be over.

I hadn't been home for a month when I found myself spiraling down into the depths of a real depression, lonely and angry with myself. Here I'd had it all—a good job, mak-

ing good money, an active life—and now all that was gone
for good in one terrible accidental moment.

I used to travel anywhere I wanted to; I took vacations in
Los Angeles, San Francisco, Chicago, St. Augustine, Orlando
Beach, Daytona Beach, Miami, Jamaica, Canada, Mexico,
New Mexico, even Buffalo, New York. If I wanted to go
somewhere, I bought myself a ticket and took off. If I
wanted to buy new clothes—and I love new shirts and Bally
shoes—I didn't think twice, I just bought them. Even gold
jewelry—rings, an antique watch chain, gold neck chains—I
had everything I wanted, including lots of pals, a good social
life, girlfriends, parties. I'd moved out of Far Rockaway and
into my own one-bedroom condo apartment not far from the
beach. Busy as I was, I loved to read, and always found time
for books. I was never lonely and I was never depressed.

All my life I'd been physically active. I loved sports and
even after I grew up I continued to play a lot of them—
paddleball, handball, racquetball, swimming. Ever since I
was nine years old I had studied the martial arts. I rode my
bike twenty miles a day. I always enjoyed the feeling of hard
work and hard play, of pushing myself mentally and physically.

I also used to collect military objects, especially things
having to do with Napoleon (in the army the other guys
called me "Napoleon," because I was shorter than most of
them) and I was proud of my collection. It's still displayed in
my home.

Now I was facing some bitter truths: I could no longer go
anywhere, buy anything, add to my collection, or make the
same free choices I had made before. I certainly wouldn't

be able to swim or ride my bike or play ball. I felt bound by my new handicap, imprisoned by the lack of money. Except for small disability payments, no money was coming in.

My social life had revolved around the city; I had worked in the city, and so did my friends. They were not so much friends as good-time buddies, it turned out, and now that the good times were over, they lost interest in me. I couldn't blame them. They were young; they had their own active lives to lead; and they simply didn't have time to think about me anymore, now that I couldn't keep up with them physically or financially.

But the worst thing of all was that I had no work to do. I was so proud of my work.

"I used to help build buildings, important ones, structures that would still be standing a hundred years from now," I complained to myself. "Now what am I going to do?"

"You could get a desk job," an acquaintance suggested. "A job in an office."

But a desk job wasn't for me. What would I do in an office? I had no sitting-down skills. I needed to be active, working with my hands and my muscles. I needed to be out of doors. Now there was nothing to get me out of the house. There was no reason for me to get up in the morning, no feeling of accomplishment, no satisfaction of a job done well, no good feeling of being tired in all my muscles at the end of the day. The world went on around me; my old friends all had jobs and were useful. I couldn't hold down a useful job anymore, so I felt totally useless.

I stopped traveling into Manhattan; I stopped going anywhere. Like many depressed people, I didn't want to leave the house, so I simply didn't go outdoors anymore. I sat indoors day and night, feeling sorry for myself. Nothing interested me, and I didn't want to think about my future, because all I could picture was me sitting around on my tail-bone doing zip.

At the beginning, my family would come to visit me. But I turned away from them, ashamed and bitter at being so obviously helpless.

"Do you need anything? Can we do something for you?" my sisters and Jose would ask.

"No, nothing. I don't need anything." I needed plenty, but I was too proud and too humiliated to ask for it. *Just go away*, I would tell them silently. *Go away and let me alone*. I think they must have sensed my attitude, because eventually even they stopped coming to see me. Besides, I was a bachelor and they all had plenty to do with families of their own. Among them, my three sisters and one brother have eighteen children.

Without my family, I had virtually no visitors at all. Life as I'd always known and enjoyed it had come to an end. My future now looked empty, black, and gloomy, as empty, black, and gloomy as my own state of mind.

2

GINNY FINDS A HOME

In ADDITION TO MY CONSTANT PAIN, my disastrous financial condition, and all my other reasons for depression, I was still facing the distinct and gloomy possibility that my arm would have to come off after all. As far as I was concerned right then, the best part of my life was over and done with. And I was only forty years old.

Most of my friends had disappeared, busy with their own active lives. But I still had one true friend who stuck by me, Sheilah Harris, who lives across the courtyard in the same apartment complex. Sheilah was really worried about me. She watched me going down the tubes, with no interest in life, no ambition to get up out of my chair and get going again. It was hard to shave with my left hand, so I stopped shaving. It was hard to change clothes, so I sat around in my wrinkled and dirty shirts. I, Philip Gonzalez, who used to take such pride in a neat and clean appearance, in expensive, sharply pressed clothing and brightly shined shoes, was a real mess. All I could do was wallow in my own misery.

"I'm ashamed of you," Sheilah scolded me one day, almost a month after I came home from the hospital. "Look at you! You've got to do something about yourself; you certainly can't go on like this. Get up out of that chair. We're going to get you a dog, right now."

"A dog?" What was she talking about? I couldn't believe my ears. A new pet after what had happened to Husky and Montoose? Get involved with a dog again and get my heart broken? No way! Besides, the last thing I needed now was to take on a responsibility, a living creature I'd have to feed and walk and look after.

But Sheilah knew that a new responsibility was exactly what I did need. Thinking about somebody else—even an animal—would take my mind off my own misery. So she persisted, and she wouldn't allow my negativity to stand in her way. Sheilah understood that I wasn't thinking straight; my self-pity kept getting in the way.

"A dog will be a companion for you. It will be your friend. Besides, keeping a dog will get you out of the house, because you'll have to take it out. When was the last time you stuck your nose out of this apartment?"

"I don't know. Maybe a week," I muttered, although I knew it was more than a week.

"Well, a dog has to be walked at least three times a day, so you'll *have* to get up out of that chair, whether you want to or not. It'll be good for you."

Notice that when Sheilah talked about companionship for me, she specified a dog, not a cat. Sheilah didn't care for cats at all; in fact, she'll tell you that in those days she really hated cats, loathing them to the point of not entering a room with a cat in it. Although I was partial to dogs, I was reluctant—no, afraid—to make any kind of effort, so I kept on grumbling excuses.

"How am I going to take care of a dog with only one working arm?" That's the way I was thinking then, defeated before I even set out.

"I'm not taking no for an answer," Sheilah said. "You don't have to adopt a dog, but just let me drive you to the animal shelter and at least have a look. You get yourself cleaned up, and I'll be back to get you in half an hour. Even if you don't find a dog you like, you'll at least have been out for a drive. And that's something. So *shave!*"

I did wash myself as well as I could, brushed my hair neatly, and I even managed a sort of lopsided left-handed shave. I had to admit that it made me feel somewhat better to look more like my old self. On the short drive over to the animal shelter in Sheilah's Chevy Nova I kept thinking about the problems that went along with adopting a dog. I was still feeling apprehensive about caring for a pet—how was I going to get a leash on a dog with only one working hand, and how was I going to keep it under control on a walk, and how was I going to clean up after it? Sheilah promised me that she would help out, but I knew that the primary responsibility for the dog would have to be mine, and I had no business asking Sheilah or anybody else to take it on.

Even with all these doubts, I was sort of getting used to the idea. But I was only thinking "big dog." A German shepherd, an Akita, a rottweiler, or maybe a Doberman pinscher. I thought only in terms of its being a purebred, a great-looking dog that other people would envy me for. And it would have to be a male. Big, tough masculine dogs can make good house pets, but they are also effective protection for somebody living alone, especially if that somebody is disabled. There was that negative reaction again—"disabled." That's how I kept thinking of myself, as somebody out of commission and entitled to pity.

When we got to the animal shelter, about 10:30 that morning, the attendant on duty was friendly and sympathetic. His name was Kenny Colon, and he was a tall Latino, about twenty-eight or twenty-nine years old, dressed in a tan workshirt and brown pants. He took one look at me, noticing at once that my arm was pretty banged up and in a sling. Right away he suggested that I should adopt a cat, a low-maintenance cat.

"A cat makes a nice, easy pet," Kenny told me diplomatically. Obviously he didn't want to hurt my feelings by saying out loud that I wasn't capable of looking after a dog. "They keep themselves clean and you don't have to take them out in all kinds of weather. We've got a lot of cats and kittens ready and waiting for homes."

"Cats don't do anything for me," I said, answering truthfully, never thinking that those words would one day come back to haunt me in spades.

I asked to see a big dog. Kenny shrugged and took me to a back room full of animal cages, in which were dogs and cats waiting to be adopted. There were maybe twelve or thirteen dogs. I walked from cage to cage, checking out the dogs inside, but not one of them appealed to me. The attendant looked at me with a question mark on his face, but I just shook my head.

"None of these. Sorry. Don't you have any more dogs?"

"Well, just a couple. Come with me."

He led me into a smaller room and showed me a cage where a Doberman pinscher was sharing quarters with a little dog who was lying down in the rear of the cage, tucked into a corner at the back, her face turned to the wall. I couldn't get a clear view of the little one, but what I saw of her looked to me like a German shepherd puppy, maybe about four months old. I thought, Great! I can raise this shepherd from a pup. Even though that would mean more trouble, the idea appealed to me—of having a dog who had never been anybody's but mine, who'd be loyal and affectionate only to me.

The shelter attendant told me that the Dobie had recently given birth to pups and she'd been neutered, and that the little "puppy" I saw in the cage with her was not a puppy after all, but another new mother who was a mixed breed, about a year old, and already spayed. The two dogs were sharing one cage because both of them were recovering from the same surgery. They'd been operated on only three days earlier, and they still had stitches in their bellies.

So the little pooch was not a puppy, but fully grown, a female and not even a German shepherd! Simply put, she was nothing but a mutt. Once I heard that, I lost all interest in her. She wasn't anything like the macho purebred dog I'd already decided to adopt.

"No, forget it," I said. "I don't want her. When will the Dobie be ready for adoption?" Even though the Doberman pinscher was female, too, she was a great-looking dog, and big enough for my taste.

But while I was asking the attendant about the Doberman, the little dog scrambled to her feet and came limping forward to the front of the cage. She had a lot of trouble walking, but she still came on gamely. Although she wasn't a puppy, she was young, less than a year old, and very peculiar-looking, a weird hybrid of probably Siberian husky and schnauzer. I'd never seen a dog like her anywhere. She had an attractive face, though—bright eyes, white eyebrows and whiskers, an intelligent, curious, amusing expression. But she had a long, skinny body and thin, crooked legs, which were oddly matched to the broad-shouldered front of her, like one of those little Volkswagen Beetles you used to see driving around with imitation Rolls-Royce radiators stuck on the hood.

Around her waist—if a dog can be said to have a waist—she was wearing an elastic bandage to keep her stitches from tearing open. Not a purebred specimen, by any means, but friendly and evidently courageous, too, because it obviously hurt her to walk, but it didn't stop her.

"That's strange," said Kenny the attendant. "She hasn't been moving around a lot, because she still has stitches in her from her surgery. That's the first time I've seen her get to her feet since her operation."

So we had something in common, this little dog and I. We'd both just been through major surgery, and we were both still shaky on our feet. She had stitches in her belly; I had staples in my arm.

I put the fingers of my left hand in through the bars, and she gave them an enthusiastic licking. Seeing this, Kenny the shelter attendant tried to persuade me to give her a home.

"Just take her out for a walk, sort of a test drive," Kenny suggested. "Once around the block."

"No. There's no point in it. I'm not interested in her at all. I'd rather have the other one, the Dobie."

"She's a good dog," he coaxed. "You'd be happy with her."

"I don't want her." I shook my head stubbornly.

"At least take her around the block, a short walk." You had to hand it to him; he was persistent. This little dog seemed to be his Special of the Day, from the way he was trying to push her off on me.

"Go ahead and take her out for a walk," Sheilah chimed in. "It won't kill you."

Oh, great, I thought. Now they're ganging up on me. I looked through the bars of the cage sourly. A skinny little dog. Some protection *she* would be in an emergency. But I could tell that neither Sheilah nor Kenny was going to let up on me until I broke down and took her out for a walk, so I agreed, halfheartedly. I made up my mind just to take her around the block once, and that would be it. Kenny put on her leash and I led her out of the shelter.

It was a bright, clear, sunny day in March, the kind of day that makes you think that winter might be over after all and that another spring might actually be on the way. The dog limped next to me on her leash, moving slowly, but obviously making an effort to keep up. Not that much effort was required, because I myself still had a lot of trouble walking. Both of us ached all over—what a pair we made! But the dog was obviously delighted to be out of her cage and in the brisk fresh air, and some of her pleasure communicated itself to me. The breeze felt good on my face.

We'd gone only about half a block when she stopped in her tracks. I'd just been dragging myself along, not even bothering to pay attention to her. I was eager to get this walk over with and get back to the Doberman, so when she stopped, I tugged impatiently at her leash, thinking that she was wasting my time hanging around doggy-style at some tempting fire hydrant or telephone pole.

But when I looked down at her I saw that she wasn't

sniffing at anything. She was just sitting there on the side-walk, looking up at me. Our eyes met, and when they did I felt a physical jolt, like a connection being made. A spark leaped between us as though there were electrical wires leading from her to me. I wasn't able to take my eyes off her face; I could swear she smiled at me.

That dog had the most appealing face I'd ever seen, bright and intelligent and curious and sweet, all at the same time. And something else shone from her face, something I had no words for then, but would come to know as deep wisdom, enormous kindness, and generosity of spirit. She was truly spiritual. Under her fluffy white eyebrows she had a pair of eyes that would melt a rock, eyes that were sympathetic, merry, and knowing. Just one look is all it took. *You're going to be my dog*, I thought.

I can't explain it, and I won't even try. I only know that I was hooked instantly on that sweet little face; from the moment I looked into this dog's eyes there was no way that Philip Gonzalez was going to let her go back to lie around in a shelter cage. She would have a permanent home with me. I could feel affection for her already rising up inside me. I even had the strange feeling that we had known each other before, in a different time and place.

"You're going home with me, dog," I said out loud. And she thumped her tail on the sidewalk three times, very deliberately . . . one . . . two . . . three. I don't know whether she understood my words or my tone, or only liked the sound of my voice, but those tail thumps of hers were a defi-nite signal of agreement.

I took the little mixed-breed right back to the shelter and filled out the adoption papers. Kenny was so tickled with himself and the dog and me that he was grinning from ear to ear. So was Sheilah, who'd proposed the whole business in the first place.

"You have a friend to take care of you now," she told me happily.

"I was sure you'd take her," Kenny said. "She's a great little dog." Then he told me what little he knew of my new dog's story.

HER STORY

Where she came from and who her parents were, nobody will ever know. She had originally belonged to a woman who had no money, none at all. She and her three children were on public assistance, but the welfare money the state gave her was spent on drugs, instead of being paid to her landlord for her rent. Eventually, she was evicted from her apartment for nonpayment. When the landlord went in to check on what he thought was the empty apartment he heard a noise coming from a closet. He opened the door, and there she was—a small, scruffy female dog, nursing three puppies.

The dog was emaciated, dehydrated, and close to death from starvation. The tenant had not only failed to pay her rent, she'd failed to feed her dog, and when she was finally thrown out of her apartment, she left behind the mother dog with her babies to starve and die.

When the shelter people arrived to rescue the dog, she showed them her teeth and growled, refusing to let them come near her puppies. In order to get her out of the closet, they had to use a long pole with a noose on it, and actually swing her out by her neck. The little dog and her pups were bundled up and taken to a nearby Long Island animal shelter, where they were given medical attention. Once they got her to the shelter and reunited her with her pups, the little dog calmed down, and when she'd had a good meal and a lot of water to drink, she showed how friendly and grateful she was by licking the hands of everyone who came to pet her and talk to her.

Although they kept feeding her, the dog remained quite skinny; her small body was functioning but was still in a starvation mode, and she couldn't use the calories efficiently. So she stayed thin and scruffy, which certainly didn't help her chances for adoption.

Even so, Kenny and the other shelter workers definitely saw something in this funny-looking female dog—a kind of strange charisma. They thought that her expressive face was almost irresistible; everybody who looked into her eyes fell for her. They became convinced that, mixed breed though she was, she would eventually find a home, and so they spayed her and earmarked her for adoption. Two of her puppies were adopted fairly soon, and the little mutt mother was taken away from her last remaining puppy so he could be weaned.

She was placed in a large cage with a female Doberman

pinscher who had also recently given birth to a litter of puppies. There, she awaited her destiny, never suspecting that it would be one of the strangest destinies a dog would ever experience. And there is where I found her and she found me.

When Kenny finished his story tears were standing in my eyes, and Sheilah was sniffling into a Kleenex. Here was an animal who had suffered terribly from human cruelty and neglect, but who held no grudges against the human race. Even though she'd been abused and neglected by people, she went on liking them. She'd acted affectionate toward me, and she seemed to love Kenny, who obviously loved her back. She appeared to me to be pleased with everything and everybody, and her excited, wriggling little body and wagging tail were saying that the world was a pretty wonderful place.

That was an opinion I hadn't held since my accident.

I made a ten-dollar donation to the animal shelter and filled out the adoption papers. Kenny gave me a leash for the dog, and loaded me up on snacks that the little dog liked, those sample packages that manufacturers give to animal shelters. Since I didn't have the use of my right hand, he fastened her new leash to her collar, and we were ready to go. The entire excursion had taken no more than three-quarters of an hour, only forty-five minutes to change my life so radically. Who could have guessed? On our way out the door, my new dog stopped at a cage where her last remaining puppy was waiting for adoption. She kissed him good-bye, giving him a final washing with her tongue. I could tell this little dog had a pretty good idea that she'd never see her puppy again, because she washed him all over, from top to bottom, three whole times. And she never did see him again, because that pup soon found a home of his own.

As soon as she climbed into Sheilah's car, the dog hopped into my lap and nestled tightly against me. She stuck her muzzle up under the seat belt and tucked it under my chin. All the way home in the car, my new pet cuddled with me. She was convincing me that she, too, knew she was going to be my dog.

Sheilah collects Ginny dolls, something like Barbie dolls, and so in honor of my friend I named the little dog Ginny. She seemed to like and understand the name, because she responded to it right away, with tail thumpings and face lickings. It didn't occur to me, when I brought her up the stairs to my apartment for the first time, that my life was about to be changed totally and forever by this abandoned pup, and that it would take a new direction I had never in my wildest dreams thought it would.

It also didn't occur to me then that, as unusual as Ginny looked from the outside, she was a hundred times more unusual on the inside; that she was, in fact, possessed of a gift that could only have come from heaven.

Dogs are well known for their affection, loyalty, friendship, even heroism. Ginny has a full share of all of these, but she has, and is, something more, as I was to find out before too long.

GINNY COMES HOME

As soon as I got her inside, Ginny ran around my one-bedroom apartment, checking out her new home. She seemed to like what she saw; at least she made no complaint. She was still tuckered out from the excitement of new people and a new place, coming on the heels of her major operation. So the first thing she did was to take a long drink of water from the dish I set down for her, and when she had lapped her fill, she curled up on the sofa and took a short nap.

For a while I just sat next to her, watching her sleep and thinking about how I was going to care for her with only one usable arm. Somehow the prospect wasn't quite as daunting now that I had Ginny as it had been before I found her. Married couples who talk about having children worry about changing messy diapers. Couples who have children just change messy diapers without thinking twice about it. Small problems have a way of shrinking to nothing when you love someone.

As I looked at her, sleeping so soundly and with such trust in a strange place, it occurred to me that we had many things in common, Ginny and I. We were both vulnerable, we had both been badly hurt, and we were both still in a recovery period. But Ginny had been hurt perhaps even more deeply than I, because my pain was due to a mindless accident while hers came out of deliberate neglect and cruelty to a defenseless animal. Yet she held no bitterness in her heart; her personality was still friendly and outgoing. Ginny still loved and trusted the human race, which she made very clear by her immediate attachment to me.

There was a message in there somewhere; I sensed it, even if I wasn't yet ready to deal with it. In my present frame of mind, who knew how much time it would take before her enthusiasm for life could begin to rub off on me?

I also realized that for only the second time in my life I had taken on the full responsibility for another living being. Sylvia the cat belonged to all the Gonzalezes; Husky had been shared among my brothers Jose and Peter and me; Sheba and Sophie had been my girlfriend's cats, and after we broke up I didn't keep them long. Only Montoose had been totally my pet, and the poor thing hadn't lived very long. And I hadn't exactly chosen Montoose; he'd sort of fallen into my hands.

But Ginny was different; she was all mine. I had chosen her (actually, she had chosen me) and her health, well-being, and happiness now all depended on me.

She slept for about an hour. When she woke up, I gave her some of the snacks I'd brought home. I thought about taking Ginny out for our first real walk together. It made me a little anxious; could I keep control of a lively young animal on a leash? But I recognized that it was time for me to begin developing the use of my left arm and hand anyway. I would be getting physical therapy on my right arm as soon as it healed, but there was no reason for me to have two useless hands in the meantime. So caring for Ginny would be doing me some physical good. It would be a form of therapy; I'd be getting used to doing things with my hands again.

Since she was still wearing her leash, I thought I'd better take her for a walk right away, to get both of us accustomed to the new regimen. Even though the neighborhood was entirely strange to her, and filled with exciting new smells and sights to investigate, Ginny limped slowly and happily along next to me, without pulling on her leash or trying to get away, exactly as though we were old friends out for a stroll, side by side.

The air was fresh on my face, and the sun was shining. It was good to be out of doors. I was feeling a whole lot better already. Walking along with Ginny already seemed the most natural thing in the world. It was as if we'd both been sprung free from our cages.

= 3 =
GINNY FINDS
A CAT

ONCE SHE ARRIVED at my apartment, Ginny made herself at home right away. The little pooch didn't seem to be timid or afraid of anything, but she was very curious. She moved slowly and with some difficulty from room to room, checking everything out with her eyes and nose. She examined every stick of my furniture, she peeked behind the curtains and sniffed in every corner, yet all the while she kept looking over her shoulder to make sure I was still there, still just behind her.

I was there every time she looked for me. It occurred to me that Ginny might get lonely on her first night in her new home. Tonight would be the first time in a long time that she would be without the company of at least one other animal. In the shelter, she had her puppies and, when they were weaned, the company of the Doberman. Now she was in a one-dog apartment with only me instead of an animal pal. But when bedtime came, Ginny seemed very willing to accept me as a substitute for her furry friends. From the first night, Ginny slept on my bed, and she shadowed me everywhere, even to the bathroom when I showered. But she always stayed away from my hurt arm, as though she knew it was still painful and too sensitive to be touched.

The day after I brought Ginny home, I could see blood showing around her stitches. Sheilah and I took her to the veterinarian in Sheilah's Chevy. This was the same vet, affiliated with the animal shelter, who had spayed Ginny a few days earlier.

I was nervous that Ginny would remember her surgery and be afraid of the doctor; maybe she would get upset. Nothing could have been further from the truth. She came in saying hello to everybody, wagging her tail with enthusiasm and kissing everyone within reach of her tongue. This was the first time I saw how strangers respond to Ginny; she adores being the focus of attention, and people seem to warm naturally to her, as she does to them. As for the blood around her bandage, it was nothing serious, and she was given some antibiotics.

The second day I had Ginny, we were out for our walk and I saw a guy walking two big dogs—a German shepherd and a rottweiler mix. I saw them coming straight at me, and I froze, thinking they were going to go for me. I dropped Ginny's leash, so she could get away. But instead of going for me, the dogs went after her, and she ran. I found out later that she ran all the way home, and that one of my neighbors opened the front door for her so she could get into the hall. But Ginny didn't want to go in. She kept looking around and making whimpering noises.

"She looked exactly like she forgot something, and she took off like a bat out of hell," my neighbor told me later.

Ginny ran all the way back to me—I was halfway home when we met on the street. Since I'd had her less than two days, I wasn't even sure she knew where we lived. But Ginny was a lot smarter than I figured; she already had the map to our house imprinted on her brain. I still think she came back to rescue me. As it turned out, Ginny wasn't at all afraid of large dogs.

It took a little while before Ginny completely forgot the cruelty that had been shown to her before she was rescued. Sheilah and I brought her home in March and she was then about a year old. My own birthday is April 1, so we gave Ginny the same birthday, and on April 1 Sheilah bought a cake and the three of us had a little party to celebrate her "first" birthday—at least, her first with me.

Sheilah cut pieces of cake for the three of us. But Ginny sidled up to the table and "stole" her piece, wolfing it down, and she then cringed on the floor, looking up at us in fear.

We realized that the poor dog had probably been forced to steal scraps of food from her former owners in order to survive. Her lowly, fearful posture and the terror in her eyes told us that she must have been punished harshly for it. It was a sad sight to see.

I resolved then and there that Ginny would never know anything but affection and a full belly from then on. I promised myself that I would erase her former fears from her memory forever.

Although I loved her from the beginning, I came to love my Ginny more and more with every day that passed. She was a wonderful, affectionate little pet and smart as the dickens. Her large, bright eyes noticed everything; she was very responsive, both to my voice and my gestures. She loved me, her "father," and adored Sheilah, her "mother." Also, Ginny seemed unusually sensitive, more sensitive than your average dog. Take, for example, her behavior with small children.

Like many dogs, Ginny is good with children and loves them, but when she sees one, she gets down on her belly and approaches them in a cringing posture, her tail wagging furiously. To anybody who knows dog body language, cringing is a clear signal of nonthreatening behavior; the dog is saying that she presents no possible danger, that she is an "underdog," and that the little baby human is in the dominant position, "so don't be afraid of me." The first September after I got Ginny, we were going for a walk, and there were pre-K children waiting for the school bus. It was the first day of school. As soon as she saw the kids, Ginny

got down on her belly and began doing the Ginny-crawl, her tail going like a windmill. The excited little boys and girls all crowded around her.

"What's his name, mister?"

"Ginny, and he's a she. Don't crowd her too close."

But the children didn't listen. They all reached out their hands to stroke her at once. "Ginny. Ginny!"

And she loved it; she couldn't get enough of their petting. We stayed until the bus came, and she never grew impatient for one second. She sopped up the petting like a furry sponge. When the children climbed onto the yellow school bus, Ginny looked as though she'd lost her best friend. After that day, she made me walk her past the bus stop every morning as a regular thing, for her stroking sessions with the children. I didn't know how to explain to her about weekends and school vacations, but she wore a disappointed look any morning that her kids weren't at the bus stop. Now they're in the third grade, and they still see Ginny and call to her and pet her.

"Ginny! There's our friend! How are you, Ginny?" And her tail wags so hard it almost lifts her off the ground.

Ginny and I went for walks several times a day, but we often also went out late at night. When I was working in construction I had to get up really early in the morning— sometimes as early as 4:00 A.M.—to be on the job site, and old habits die hard. I enjoy the solitude of the small hours of the morning. The streets are dark and quiet at 3:30 or 4:00, and in my neighborhood they are peaceful. Sometimes, but not often, we'd see other dog-walkers out late, but there were always stray cats, hiding in the alleys, scrounging for food in the garbage pails, taking shelter wherever they could find it in rough weather. Feral cats are creatures of the night.

I soon noticed that whenever we'd take our walks Ginny would pull on her leash at the sight of a homeless cat. She'd try to get at it, wanting to get closer, but I always held her leash tightly in my good hand. I didn't know what her intentions were, but I knew that dogs and cats were supposed to be traditional enemies, and I was definitely not in shape to run after a dog who was chasing a cat through back alleys and vacant lots and jumping over chain-link fences.

But one night, at about 4:00 A.M., as she was straining at her collar, whimpering, I accidentally dropped the leash. As though she were an arrow shot from a bow, Ginny flew straight into a vacant lot and ran directly up to a stray cat. Before I could stop her, Ginny was nose to nose with the cat, actually licking and grooming it. And the cat, a pretty little long-haired golden kitten, was purring and rubbing against Ginny.

This certainly didn't look like the meeting of two traditional enemies. These two were acting as though they were old buddies holding a reunion.

Even so, I couldn't take any chances, so I grabbed up her leash and took Ginny back home. But she was unusually restless, crying and scratching to go back out. It occurred to me that maybe she wanted to feed that kitten. I didn't have any cat food, but I opened a can of Ginny's dog food and back we went to the vacant lot.

When I put the food down, that little yellow kitten appeared out of the shadows like magic and ate as though she were starving, which she no doubt was. But after she finished eating, she didn't run away. Instead, she stayed, and she and Ginny played like two old friends. They romped together and pretended to chase each other around the lot, but without catching each other, like a kid's game of tag. At one point the homeless cat actually hopped on Ginny's back and went for a ride! And Ginny didn't mind at all carrying the kitten on her back; she seemed to enjoy it.

So did I. It was one of the most amusing and touching sights I'd ever seen, my dog and this homeless stray having such a good time together. After watching them for half an hour or so, I led Ginny home. The next night I woke at about 3:30 A.M. to take Ginny for our late walk. We met up with our homeless pal again. Once again they touched noses and played like old buddies. She whimpered when I brought her home until I got out another can of dog food and we went back to the vacant lot, where I fed Ginny's new friend.

After that, I bought some canned cat food and carried it with me on my nightly walks with Ginny. I fed the stray every night, only our "stray" soon became our "strays." As more and more cats kept turning up to be fed, Ginny was obviously happy to see them all. I added cat food to my weekly grocery list, and bought a large number of pop-top cans and bags of crunchy dry food. It was surprising how quickly the food vanished, so I kept buying larger and larger quantities, even though it was taking a huge bite out of my workmen's comp checks.

GINNY GETS HER FIRST CAT

Ginny and I often used to go back to see her former friends at the animal shelter. Because I was so happy with her, I felt grateful to the shelter. It even occurred to me that I'd ripped them off; I'd given them only ten bucks, and they had given me in exchange a creature who was all affection, who was a good friend and great company. Ginny was the bargain of the century. In my opinion I still owed the shelter, I owed them big.

So I would buy all kinds of cat and dog snacks and take Ginny back there for a visit, and we'd give her old pals in the cages a little treat. Ginny and Kenny were always happy to see each other, and my little dog would make the rounds of the cages, saying hello to old fellow shelter-tenants who were still waiting for homes—her own puppy had been adopted soon after Ginny found her own home—and making the acquaintance of the new arrivals.

I was surprised to notice that she seemed particularly interested in the cats. She'd spend much more time at their cages than she did with the dogs. And we were still feeding stray cats at night. Not an evening went by that Ginny didn't lead me straight to that vacant lot to play with her feline friends. She was apparently a born cat-lover.

About a month after Ginny came to live with me, Sheilah Harris brought up the topic of a pet for my pet. "She must miss her puppies. Let's take her to the shelter and pick out a friend for her." Of course, Sheilah the cat-hater meant for me to get another dog.

It seemed like a good idea, so the three of us climbed into the Chevy Nova and drove back to the animal shelter to get Ginny a friend. But I didn't spend a lot of time at the dog cages. Since she liked cats so much, I had already decided to get her a kitten as a companion. Not for me, mind you, but for her; Ginny was the cat-lover, not me.

It was spring, and spring is kitten season. There must have been forty or fifty cute little kittens waiting for adoption at the shelter. The cages were filled with kittens—mewing, playing, batting at each other's ears, rolling over one another, climbing up the bars of the cage, snoozing—all of them adorable, all of them waiting for good homes.

Ginny ran eagerly from cat cage to cat cage until she saw a very pretty kitten, snow white with big blue eyes, about ten weeks old. The kitten was a real knockout; she looked like something you'd see on a valentine card, fluffy and very cuddly. It was obvious that from the minute she laid eyes on the kitten, this was the one Ginny wanted. She began to whimper and actually tried to climb into the cage. I opened the cage door, took the kitten out, and handed her to Ginny. Right away, she began to clean and groom it, exactly like a mother cat. She licked it vigorously, she even

nibbled its fur gently with her teeth, the same way a mother cat does. The kitten loved it and showed her approval by purring loudly.

I adopted the white kitten for Ginny and named her Madame. Two days after I took her home, I realized that something was wrong with the kitten. She was affectionate and responsive when she was looking straight at me, but when her eyes were closed, or her back was toward me, she paid no attention to me or my voice. When I spoke her name, her ears didn't even twitch. Most important, when I opened a can of cat food in the kitchen, or rattled her food dish, she didn't come running, even though the electric can opener is the best cat caller ever invented. I had my suspicions, so I walked up behind her and clapped my hands, loud.

Madame didn't cock her ears or turn her head toward the sound. She didn't even flinch; she was stone deaf! I found out later that there is a gene for deafness in white cats with blue eyes, which is why you often see a pure white cat with one blue eye and one yellow or green eye. This is nature's way of protecting the animal against deafness. Usually, deafness will surface in male cats, but in the case of Madame it was a female who was born deaf.

What happens is this: a cat's hearing depends on a structure in the inner ear called the cochlea, which in a hearing cat secretes a special fluid used by the cat's organ of Corti. The organ of Corti takes sound vibrations and transmits them to the brain, where they are turned into sounds, but it needs that special fluid to do the job. In a white, blue-eyed cat like Madame, often the fluid dries up soon after its birth and is never secreted again. The organ of Corti then degenerates and sound vibrations cannot be carried to the cat's brain. The entire sound-transmission mechanism has broken down, and the damage is permanent and incurable.

From all the kittens available in our local animal shelter, Ginny had selected a handicapped cat to save and cherish. I had no way of knowing it back then, but a lifetime pattern was already being set.

I enjoyed watching Ginny as she raised Madame from a kitten. She behaved exactly like a mother cat; she gave up sleeping on my bed and slept instead curled around the kitten, who nestled against her belly, purring loudly, her little paws making bread in the air. I gave them a cardboard box with an old sweater of mine spread out on the bottom to make the box warm and snug, and the two of them used it for a bed. Several times a day, Ginny would groom tiny Madame with her tongue and with the gentle tips of her teeth, and she always watched over the cat when she ate. She never let that kitten out of her sight.

I could swear that Ginny understood that Madame was deaf. She would never approach the kitten from the rear, but always circled around to the front where the kitten could see her. She never barked at her, either; it was as though she knew that Madame couldn't hear her barking.

But the funniest thing was the way Ginny moved Madame around. At first, when the kitten was really small, Ginny would carry her from place to place in her mouth, exactly as a mother cat would. She held Madame gently in her teeth by the loose fur on the back of her neck, and the kitten would dangle, paws in the air, her eyes squeezed tightly shut and her little tail curled up on her belly. She seemed to enjoy being carried, because you could hear her purring in the next room.

But in a couple of months, Madame had grown too big and too heavy for Ginny to carry around, so Ginny took to pushing the kitten across the floor with her nose, exactly like the puck in a game of shuffleboard. Anywhere Ginny wanted Madame to go, she pushed her. The kitten would close her eyes and allow herself to be pushed, as though she thought it was all a game. Ginny kept this up until Madame was full-grown. It was a truly comical sight to see a little white cat gliding across the floor at the end of a dog's nose.

By the time she was three months old, Madame had learned to compensate for her deafness. Nature is wonderful, and nature provided that little white cat with special senses. Her eyesight is spectacular, even for a cat, and she possesses a sense of smell so highly developed that I swear she can smell the cat food right through the can.

Madame has a real sweet tooth for Tender Vittles, which comes double-packaged in sealed paper pouches inside a box. I don't buy it often, and I feed it to her only as an occasional treat, but whenever I have some in my grocery bag, Madame will be sitting at the front door waiting for me. Tender Vittles days are the only occasions on which she honors me that way. She must be able to smell it right through the box, all the way from the supermarket.

In time, Madame learned to "hear" with her body. Although she could never distinguish voices, she could tell if somebody was walking toward her because of the vibrations in the floor. And, perhaps because she lives in a world of profound silence, she is a peaceful and nonaggressive cat, sweet-natured, affectionate, but not exactly of a calm disposition. When she was a young cat, she was a holy terror. Not to people, but to my furniture and possessions.

Madame would swing through the air like Tarzan, leaping from curtain to curtain, tearing them with her claws. She was death to china, lamps, even the poor old VCR, which she landed on from a height of eight feet in the air and knocked down off its table. And she loved to disappear; it was her favorite game. One of her best tricks was to poke a small hole in the cambric underlining of my sofa, enlarge the hole with her paw until it was big enough for her to climb into, and there she would hide, hanging inside the sofa bottom, up off the floor, unseen, as though she were swinging in her own private hammock.

Another time when she was still a kitten, Madame vanished off the face of the earth for more than two hours. I looked high and low for her, with no success. And she couldn't hear me calling, not that hearing would have made any difference. When a cat wants to hide out, it can make itself selectively deaf, even if it wasn't born deaf.

I was at my wit's end. I couldn't remember whether I'd

had the front door of my apartment open for a few minutes. If Madame had wandered out, she'd be at a terrible disadvantage. A deaf cat has no business being out on the street; it has no natural defenses against hundreds of possible dangers, like speeding cars or dogs that are not in its line of vision. Automobiles are statistically the nation's biggest killer of cats.

Ginny trotted in from the bedroom, where she had been napping.

"Ginny, go find Madame," I said, not knowing whether or not it would work. But Ginny understands everything; she went straight to the lamp table next to the sofa. There was a lamp on it that Madame had knocked over once and broken a hole in, but because I couldn't afford a new lamp I'd put the shade back on it and turned the hole away toward the wall.

Ginny went up to the lamp and put her paw on it, tapping it twice. At once, little Madame came out of the hole. She had curled up inside the hole, under the lampshade, because the lamp was lit and she enjoyed the heat it generated. The vibrations from Ginny's tapping paw woke her up and brought her out.

Madame and Ginny still have a special relationship; Ginny will defend Madame if any of the other cats try to pick on her, and Madame will still cuddle up against Ginny from time to time, as if asking to be groomed. Ginny, of course, is always happy to oblige, and nibbles and licks Madame's fur.

VOGUE AND REVLON

Not long after we adopted Madame, Sheilah and I were walking Ginny during the day and she began to bark, really loud, and strain at her leash, so I let her pull me in the direction she seemed to want to go. When we turned the corner, we saw a group of people—adults—mercilessly kicking around a homeless cat. They were actually using this poor creature as some kind of football. Ginny got very excited and upset, and began to bark her head off, something she rarely does.

I realized that she had literally dragged me into this situation so that I could do something about it. I couldn't stand to watch such cruelty to a helpless animal, so I grabbed up the cat and took her out of there. Sheilah drove her to my veterinarian's office to be patched up, given shots, and spayed. I thought that we might be able to find a good home for her. The vet said she wasn't a kitten, but probably seven or eight years old. That's a pretty long time for a cat to survive out on the street, so there was a good chance that she had been a house pet or maybe a store cat who had fallen on hard times and become homeless.

But when we brought her home, it turned out to be for keeps. This was Vogue, Ginny's second cat. At first, Vogue was leery of everything and everybody, and you couldn't blame her for being paranoid, considering what she'd gone through. She cowered in a corner of my apartment and didn't want to come out, not even to eat. She hissed at me, at Ginny, and at the little kitten Madame. She didn't seem to like any of us.

But Ginny didn't give up on her. She went on coaxing her in that special way of hers, by staying near Vogue, keeping very quiet and supportive, and, whenever the cat would permit it, giving her a tongue bath. Before the week was over, Vogue was reassured that she had finally arrived in a safe place, so she slowly began to venture out of her corner. The strange thing was that, although I expected Vogue would become Ginny's baby, it actually happened the other way around. Ginny became Vogue's baby, and Vogue was always checking up on her, licking and grooming Ginny, holding her down with a paw, and staying close to her like a mother cat with one kitten.

One night, when I was sleeping, I felt a weight on my chest and woke up. When I opened my eyes, there was Vogue, making herself comfortable on my chest. After that night, she joined our little family and became a special pet to me, sleeping in my bed, tucked under the covers, snuggled up against me, until her death from cancer three years later. I still miss her.

I finally decided that Vogue might have been an office cat in her earlier life, because she loved to mess with equipment and buttons, especially buttons. She was fascinated by the buttons of the telephone, and she would always play with them. Once she made a long-distance call. She must have knocked the receiver off the hook by rubbing against it—I saw her do that more than once—and at

the same time pressed a button that speed-dialed my
brother Jose, who's now living in Miami. When Jose
answered the phone, he could hear mewing and purring,
but no conversation. Still, he figured out that the call must
have come from my house and we had a good laugh about
it later. But I kept a watchful eye on my phone bill after
that; I didn't want Vogue making calls to Belgium, Angola,
Taipei, or New Zealand, or phoning to order a pizza with
everything on it.

About two weeks after we got Vogue, we made our usual
visit to the shelter again, just to say hello to Kenny and feed
treats to the animals. Ginny ran right up to a cat cage and
began that increasingly familiar whimpering that seemed to
be saying, "Please . . . gimme . . . gimme . . . gimme that
cat."

I looked into the cage and saw a really scruffy and dirty
orange cat. I'd noticed this cat before, but it always kept
turned away to the wall, facing the back of its cage, and I'd
never seen its face. But with Ginny whimpering at it, the
cat finally turned around. It was a female, with one good
eye and one that was totally messed up. She had obviously
been mistreated before someone turned her into the shelter.

"Come on, Ginny, you already have two cats at home," I
protested. "Two's plenty, so just let up, please."

But Ginny wouldn't let up, she just kept whimpering and
trying to get at the little cat. Of course I had to give in. I
couldn't refuse my dog anything, even another cat with a
bad eye. So I adopted her out of the shelter. Ginny couldn't

wait to groom and clean her; the red cat was dirty and looked terrible. Sheilah and I took her to the vet. She was about five months old and in pretty sorry shape. One eye was swollen shut and oozing.

"This eye can't be saved," the vet said. "It will have to come out, or the infection will most likely spread to her brain and kill her. Or, if you'd rather, we can put her to sleep right now."

Of course, I couldn't let that happen. Ginny would never forgive me. I agreed to the surgery, and when she had healed enough to be ready to come home, I knew that she was going to live with us. It was what Ginny wanted. Because she was red like lipstick, I named her Revlon. So now Ginny had a third cat, another rescued stray, and yet another cat with a disability. Having only one eye didn't seem to slow Revlon down any. She was a wild child, playful and teasing.

Later, when there were more cats in the Ginny/Gonzalez household, Revlon showed us that she didn't care for male cats at all, even if all of them were neutered, which of course all my cats were and are. "No men" was her motto. She would tease the males, Caesar, Solomon, and Napoleon, luring them to her with flirtatious behavior. Then, when they got within paw's reach, she'd whip out and give them a smack in their faces. Oddly, they didn't seem to mind getting their ears boxed, so the gullible boys kept falling over and over again for the wild redhead's enchanting tricks.

✿　　　✿　　　✿

So there it was. I had adopted a dog, and the dog had adopted three cats for herself. One of the cats had been cruelly abused, and two came complete with physical disabilities. But that didn't matter to either of us; Ginny loved them anyway. And I discovered that I couldn't be indifferent to cats anymore. They were beginning to purr their way into my heart, and were now mine as well as Ginny's.

= 4 =
BETTY BOOP AND THE GANG

LOOKING BACK over the last few years, I think that it was right after Ginny and I got our first three cats that my life began to take the strange turn that it did. Up until that time, I guess I expected that I would someday go back to my old existence, or at least as much of my old existence as my damaged arm would permit. Day by day I was getting stronger, regaining a little use of my right hand, although it was limited use and I was still on medication. Even today, I have only about 20 percent use of that hand. When I walk through the streets, I carry my right arm underneath my jacket, so that nobody can tell it's not a working arm. It's a lot safer that way, especially when people don't want you to rescue homeless cats. Sometimes they get a little . . . emphatic . . . and it's best if they think you've got two good, strong functioning hands. I imagined I'd be getting a job again, maybe not in construction, but still the kind of job where I'd be earning a decent living. I thought of it as getting back to normal. What I didn't expect was that my life would never again be the same as before my accident; instead, my feet would be traveling down an entirely new path, and a pretty surprising path, too.

If I believed that my little family was now complete with a dog and three cats, I could not have been more wrong. Although I didn't recognize it back then, my life had reached a definite turning point, thanks to Ginny.

It all started—big surprise!—with another cat. One day I took Ginny over to the vet's for her scheduled shots, and there was a cat in his office, a gray-and-white with a rope around her neck. Some kids had found her abandoned in the street, and had brought her in for the doctor to help her.

Immediately, Ginny was drawn to this new cat, like iron filings to a magnet. She began to make her "please, please, gimme, gimme" noises, and I knew that if Ginny wanted this cat something had to be wrong with it. Sure enough, the little cat had no back feet at all, and only half a tail.

Another real winner. I held tightly to Ginny's leash. This one she wasn't going to bring home, I resolved.

"How did she lose her back feet?" I asked the vet.

"It's hard to say. Frostbite, maybe, but there's a chance she was born that way. Philip, let me warn you. Don't go near her. She's pretty wild, and she could easily bite your finger off."

"What are you going to do with her?" I had absolutely no intentions toward this wretched creature, but I was curious.

The veterinarian shook his head. "I don't know yet. Maybe I'll have to put her out of her misery. Nobody in his right mind would give this cat a home."

The doctor was right. You had to be stone crazy to take this cat in, and Mother Gonzalez didn't raise any crazy children. But if I had no intentions, Ginny most certainly did. For some reason, she fell instantly in love with this ferocious crippled puss. As soon as my hand relaxed on her leash, Ginny ran up to her with that old familiar whimpering, and before I could pull her away, she was grooming this decrepit wildcat, paying no attention to her hisses of protest. The cat's eyes were flashing danger signals, but Ginny blissfully ignored them. She turned back to me, put her head to one side, and gave me that old familiar "I have to have this cat, you have to give me this cat" whimper again and again.

"Oh, no, Ginny, not this time. No way." Not another cat, especially not this one. Mean temperament and no back feet? Uh-uh. Enough was enough. I shook my head firmly. My word was absolute law. After all, Ginny was only the dog. I was the master, right?

Wrong. This was a handicapped cat, and you know Ginny

and handicapped cats. She wanted her, bad, and she was out-and-out determined to get her. Speaking of "out," I was outvoted and probably outsmarted, too, because the next thing I knew, we were taking the rope off the animal's neck and putting the furious cat, who hadn't stopped hissing, spitting, and cursing in cat language, into a carrier.

Against my better judgment, I took her home to my apartment. Or should I say Ginny's apartment—since she was the one who seemed to dictate who would live in it. I named the new cat Betty Boop.

I never expected this wildcat to be a member of our family, but once again, Ginny proved to be right and I was wrong. It took Betty Boop a few weeks to adjust, but eventually her paranoia did dissolve, and it was replaced by an outpouring of the purest love. It was as though for the first time floodgates of affection were opened in the little cat's soul. One night, I woke up to find her lying on my chest with her front paws folded under her body, purring away happily. After that, Betty Boop slept on my bed every night, together with Vogue, who befriended her. And some nights Ginny and Madame slept there, too. She soon began to return Ginny's open affection. The two of them became best friends and are still best friends.

As for her disability—after a few weeks I stopped noticing that Betty Boop was missing her hind feet. Although she couldn't move gracefully like a cat, she managed to hop around like a rabbit, so she always did get to anywhere she wanted to go.

The amount of love in that little cat's heart is something miraculous. In our home, she serves as a peacemaker. If two cats are hissing at each other, or thinking about having a fight, Betty Boop pushes her way between them and convinces them to stop quarreling. Ginny does that, too, but Ginny can't be everywhere at once.

After Betty Boop joined the family, I began to get a real understanding of Ginny's devoted commitment and her unique talent for finding cats, especially disabled cats. As hard as it was to believe at first, my dog seemed to be on a special mission, to rescue homeless animals who would otherwise suffer and die. I became convinced that she had been chosen from above for the task, and she had chosen me to help her complete it. I say it was hard to accept at the beginning, but soon Ginny's miraculous abilities became to me the most natural thing in the world. It also began to give my day-to-day life a real sense of purpose.

More than merely having compassion for creatures in trouble, Ginny actually sought out these animals to make their lives better. And those objects of this angelic dog's compassion were cats: stray cats, starving cats, ill cats, and especially, physically handicapped cats. Ginny's heart goes out in love to those cats who need her, and she rescues them from their miserable lives.

Just as she rescued me from mine.

Ginny's favorite food is what New Yorkers call "appetizing." Mostly, appetizing refers to pickled or smoked fish, like lox, or whitefish, baked salmon—her number one favorite—herring, or sable. But it also includes bagels, cream cheese, pickles, sour tomatoes, and even delicatessen. Ginny—as well as most New Yorkers—loves all that stuff with a passion, but she doesn't get it often because it's so high in salt and fat. But every now and then I give her a treat because she enjoys it so much that I haven't got the heart to keep it from her. It's little enough to repay her for what she has done for me.

As I told you, Vogue developed cancer. In her last days, Betty Boop never left Vogue's side. She stayed by her constantly, licking and grooming and comforting her. It was as though she knew that Vogue was dying, and she wanted to make the end as comfortable as possible. Vogue wouldn't let any of the other cats even come near her; the only two presences she could tolerate were Ginny and Betty Boop.

I said that Betty Boop was the turning point because after her I became Ginny Gonzalez's full partner and accomplice in saving homeless cats from destruction. I think what happened is that I finally saw clearly what my dog Ginny had been trying to show me all along: that animals with disabilities are just as deserving of homes as animals who are intact, even more so, because their needs are greater. We now had a deaf cat, a half-blind cat, and a cat who hopped around like a rabbit, and they were all wonderful, loving, lovable pets.

That's not to say I didn't have doubts from time to time. I can't claim that I was converted by Ginny on the spot, or never again tried to turn away from cat rescue; I did. The direction my life seemed to be taking was often frightening. After I brought home an entire litter of five newborn kittens, I had a stern talk with myself.

"Just what do you think you are doing?" I demanded of Philip Gonzalez. "You haven't got a dime to your name, you're living on workmen's compensation, and meanwhile you're laying out a fortune on cat food and vet bills. That's gotta be the craziest thing anybody ever did. A dog and a couple of cats, sure. That's normal, nothing wrong with that. But here you are, in a one-bedroom apartment overflowing with felines, trying to rescue every homeless cat on Long Island, and you're never satisfied unless you are feeding dozens of cats a day. What are you, nuts? How long can insanity like this go on? When are you going to wise up? What kind of future is there in stuff like this?"

There was a lot of common sense in my questions to myself. They were hard questions, but there was an answer. The answer had been in my soul all along. And it was this:

Being a casual kind of guy, I was no philosopher. I had never looked into my heart or examined my life. I'd always accepted everything that happened to me one day at a time, as the cards were dealt from the deck. Not once had I ever asked myself, "Why am I here? What is the meaning of my life? Does God have something special in mind for me to do?" Now it seemed to me that He did, and that my little dog Ginny had been given to me as God's own instrument. Ginny was pointing the way for me by her own shining examples of caring and mercy.

Nothing I had ever done in my life had afforded me the same sense of satisfaction, of rightness, that going on rescue missions with Ginny had given me. Nothing had ever made me so happy, or given me such a sense of purpose, or boosted my self-esteem. Before I got Ginny, all I could do was wallow in self-pity, and regret that I had no work to do.

Now I had a job, and it was the best and most meaningful job I'd ever held in my life. I was Philip Gonzalez, rescuer of cats, Ginny Gonzalez's good left hand. Ginny had been sent into this world with a special gift, and she was sharing that gift with me.

With Ginny to guide me, I began to devote all my waking hours to finding homes for cats. At that time we were feeding about thirty street cats, and one by one I would pick them up and take them to the vet. They'd get their inoculations against killer diseases like rabies, feline leukemia, distemper, and feline AIDS, and they would be neutered. Then, if I couldn't get them adopted, I would return them to their street life. But at least they would now be healthy and wouldn't make more unwanted cats, and I continued to feed them. So their lives were a lot better than before Ginny and I came on the scene.

Our little family was growing by leaps and bounds, and so were my expenses. I was spending every penny I could spare on cat food and vet bills. The veterinarian was kind enough to slash his fees to the bone, but the expense still took a healthy bite out of my tiny income. I was now not only feeding some thirty homeless cats every day, plus my own indoor animals, but I was also paying for their medical attention, shots, neuterings, and, whenever possible, finding them homes.

I still wasn't working, and I was living only on my disability check, but even when money was scarce, somehow I always found enough for cat and dog food. If there was no money at all, I sold something. Bit by bit, I sold off all my gold jewelry, even the antique watch and watch chain that I was so fond of, to buy cat food. I took a loss on the jewelry, because you can never get its real value when you sell it. And I started to think, "Why did I take all those trips and buy all those clothes? I could have all that money now to use for cat food and vet fees."

It didn't occur to me then, but those thoughts were hard evidence of the changes I was going through, thanks to Ginny. Before, I had lived totally for myself, with no responsibilities. Now my little dog (well, not so little anymore, because now she was up to about thirty-two pounds) was showing me that living for others was a better way.

Knowing that Ginny and her puppies had nearly starved to death, that homeless cats were starving and freezing every night in the streets, made me very conscious of how often helpless animals are abused, and that people can and should do something about it.

What I did about it was give a warm and loving home to disabled cats who in the normal course of events would never find a home. And what Ginny did was to find these cats for me to rescue. We were a team.

TOPSY JOINS THE GANG

With Madame, Revlon, Vogue, and Betty Boop, I honestly thought that Ginny and I had enough cats. But Ginny clearly did not. She was beginning to make it plain that, as long as there was breath in her body, and as long as there was a cat out there who needed an extra helping of love and understanding, as long as there was an abused cat, an injured cat, a disabled cat, a disfigured cat, a cat in trouble or in pain, Ginny would find it with her special radar and compel me to help.

One night we were walking near a building under construction, and Ginny began her old familiar whimpering. The only time she whimpers like that is when there's a cat to rescue or a little child to play with. I couldn't see or hear anything, but Ginny obviously did. She kept tugging at her leash, straining to reach the construction site.

Sheilah was with me, and we weren't sure of what to do, but both of us trusted Ginny's instincts completely. If she said there was a cat somewhere in the building, there had to be a cat. Ginny was never wrong. We saw a security guard in charge of the construction site and approached him for permission to go into the building under renovation.

"There's nothing in there, guaranteed," he protested. "I would have seen it or heard it, if there was a cat in there."

But Ginny wouldn't take no for an answer, and the security guard melted and gave in when he saw her large, pleading eyes. She had that effect on a lot of people who discovered they couldn't say no to her. The security guard unlocked the gate, I dropped Ginny's leash, and into the empty building she dashed at top speed.

Sheilah and I followed her. It was pretty rough going. The floors were covered in construction rubble, mostly cement. We couldn't see anything alive or moving. But in a few minutes, Ginny came trotting back to us, carrying a tiny kitten gently in her mouth, just like a mother cat. She dropped the little cat at our feet. The kitten was all dusty, and its fur was the same color as cement, perfect camouflage. Yet Ginny had found her, trapped in an air-conditioning duct.

We followed Ginny back to the duct and there we saw not one, but several cat mothers with kittens. As soon as they spotted us, the mothers scattered in panic, each one carrying a kitten in her mouth. They weren't afraid of Ginny, but the sight of me and Sheilah terrified them. Considering that we'd been told, "There's nothing in there, guaranteed," there was a lot of living going on in that location.

The kitten Ginny had rescued was the only disabled cat of all the litters. She was a real mess. There was a huge scab on her lower jaw, all the way around her face, and she couldn't even close her mouth. More important, she couldn't walk or even stand up, and my first thought was that she had fallen from the roof and been injured, so we rushed her to the all-night veterinarian's office we use in nocturnal emergencies.

The vet examined her, and said, "She's six weeks old."

Sheilah and I looked at each other, astonished. Six weeks! The kitten was so small and feeble we thought she couldn't be more than a few days old.

"She's very sick," the vet added. He determined that she had been born with hypoplasia cerebella, a brain disorder, and she would never be able to walk. She was totally brain-damaged. He advised me to have her put to sleep, but Ginny, glued to the kitten's side, wouldn't allow it. And neither, I realized, would I.

That's how Topsy joined our family. She can't walk, she can't even stand up, yet she manages to get around and even to use her litter box. How she does it is incredible to see. She rolls. She rolls herself along the floor and even up and over the edge of her litter box. Topsy's survival is something of a medical miracle. Hypoplasia cerebella is a rare congenital defect, so rare it's not listed in any of my cat care books. Cats with this defect cannot possibly survive into a normal life, and veterinarians usually immediately put such kittens to sleep.

But Topsy is, I said, a miracle cat. To me she embodies every bit of magic in Ginny's power. If ever a kitten seemed to have two strikes against her and be marked for destruction, Topsy was it. But God didn't want to let her die, so He sent His secret weapon, Ginny, and Ginny took me along with her.

Maybe Topsy will never compete in the Cat Olympics, but her quality of life is excellent, especially for a cat with her disability. She has food, shelter, medical attention, and most important, she has love.

Of all our cats, Topsy gets the most special care. She plays with all her toys, she has her own little cat house, which she enjoys. She rolls in and out of it, and takes naps there. When she's used her litter box, I lift her out and clean her off. To me she seems to be the happiest cat in the place. I call her my "Precious One," because she is so special. But she bites. If you put your fingers anywhere near her face, such as when you try to pat her head, she'll take a sharp nip at them.

But she never, never bites Ginny.

= 5 =

RADAR OF THE HEART

It's a lot of fun to watch Ginny play with cats. She likes to herd them along like a miniature sheepdog, bossing them around, putting them into order, as though she's either their mother or a drill sergeant. She runs back and forth, counting them to make sure they're all present and accounted for. Occasionally she'll flip one over on its back so that she can groom its belly. Grooming is very high on Ginny's list of priorities; not only does it get the cats clean in places they can't reach themselves, such as their shoulder blades and the bases of their spines, but it forges a bond of care and affection between them and Ginny.

GINNY IS KIDNAPPED

Early in her career as a cat rescuer Ginny was kidnapped. I had an appointment with my allergy specialist, so I brought my animals down to Sheilah Harris's ground-floor apartment for the day. There were only four cats living with me in those days—Madame, Vogue, Revlon, and Betty Boop—and the litter of five kittens I'll tell you about in a little while. Ginny looked after them all.

Later in the day Sheilah had to go to work, and she left them alone, knowing that I'd be back soon. When I let myself into Sheilah's apartment, I knew something was wrong. The cats and kittens were upset and mewing, and Ginny was nowhere to be seen. I checked the kitchen, and I noticed right away that the window, which faced an alley, had been broken. Ginny had been snatched. Immediately, I phoned Sheilah at work to break the news to her.

We were frantic. Who could have done this? Where was she now? Was Ginny still alive? When Sheilah came home she was ready to call the police, the FBI, even the CIA. But then the telephone rang, and a young voice—more a boy's voice than a man's—said, "If you want your dog back, you've got to give us a hundred and fifty dollars."

What could we do? They obviously had Ginny. We agreed. Money was no object; all we wanted was that sweet-faced little dog home again safe and sound. Of course, I also wanted to break a couple of necks. As we'd arranged over the phone, Sheilah and I went out to meet the kidnappers. While we were driving, a garbage truck rolled by, stopped next to us at the light, and one of the sanitation men called down to me, "Are you looking for your dog?"

"Yes!" I yelled back. "Did you see her?"

"Your dog is running loose on the boardwalk."

Ginny, on the boardwalk?

"Yeah, your dog is over there, but we couldn't get at her."

"Show me where she is and I'll give you a hundred dollars."

"I'll show you where she is, Mac, but you don't have to give us a penny."

Sheilah and I followed the sanitation truck to a section of the boardwalk.

"Your dog is somewhere over there."

I got out of the car and made my way to the boardwalk. I couldn't see any sign of Ginny, but I began to call out her name, over and over. No Ginny.

"Ginny, are you playing hide-and-seek with me? Come on, girl, this isn't funny. Ginny!!"

Suddenly, I heard the welcome sound of a sharp bark, and there she was, running straight at me. I bent down and she jumped up into my arms and began to lick my face all over. I hustled her into Sheilah's car and we drove home, right after we insisted on giving those sanitation men the $100 we'd promised.

This is what we figured out: whoever stole Ginny—and I'm certain it was kids—didn't bother to take her leash. We found the leash in Sheilah's apartment. Without it, they weren't able to hold on to her, and she got away from them and started to come home. But somehow she became disoriented and stayed on the boardwalk. I think she was expecting us to turn up and find her, and we did.

Later that evening, Sheilah got another telephone call from the "kidnappers," who had no idea that Ginny was home safe and well. They probably figured she was still lost out there near the beach, and this was their last chance to get money out of us. "You didn't show up, so now you gotta pay us five hundred dollars," a very young voice said.

When Sheilah heard that, she exploded all over the telephone. She called him every name in the book, and a few that had never been listed in the book. She had a few choice phrases for his motives, his face, his friends. She called them dumb, dumber, and dumbest. And she ended up by telling him in no uncertain terms that he should get off the streets and back to school, and if he ever pulled another stunt like this, she'd have the police down on his head before Ginny could bark. By the time she was finished, Sheilah was out of breath, and the caller had blisters on his ears.

After that, we never left Ginny alone again, not even for five minutes. If Sheilah was looking after her and had to go to work, she'd drive Ginny over to her mother's, who adored Ginny and spoiled her rotten with her favorite food, baked salmon.

TIGER, SPOT, CAESAR, PINKY, AND PRINCESS

Shortly after the time we took Topsy home, I was feeding more than forty cats a day. Whenever I walked Ginny, all those strays would come out of their hiding places and walk alongside her, more than a dozen at a time. Sometimes it was just like a parade.

A man on the street stopped me once when our parade was going by. "What are you, the Pied Piper of Long Island? Why are all those cats following you?"

I laughed. "Following *me*? Just watch this." I let go of Ginny's leash, and she headed off in a different direction. And every one of those cats went after her!

Ginny and I had an agenda and a routine. We'd feed strays twice a day, and try to capture the strays we could manage, then take them to the vet for their shots and neutering. By now the doctor was giving me a quantity discount. Then I would attempt to find good homes for the cats.

It happened several times that I was taking a cat back from the vet, all neutered and inoculated and ready to go, when I'd be stopped on the street. People from the neighborhood recognized me as the crazy guy with the cats.

"What are you going to do with that cat?" someone would ask me.

"I'm looking for a home for it. It's had all its shots and it's been neutered, so it's in top condition."

"May I have it? I'll give it a good home."

I'd size the person up. "Okay, but I have to walk you home. I need the carrier, and I want to see where you live and what kind of home the cat is going to have." I wouldn't give a cat to just anybody; they had to be the right kind of people, good-natured and with loving hearts.

Up to that time, I'd placed homeless cats in more than thirty-five good homes, but there were always more abandoned cats to take their places. If I couldn't find a home for the cat, I'd release it back into its former life, but I'd still keep an eye on it and make certain it was well fed. Every adoption was a triumph for me, and every neutering was a chance to stop the production of unwanted kittens. I don't think of the street cats I feed as "strays"; I call them our "outside cats." Whenever Ginny finds a cat that has a crippled condition or a deformity that makes it unadoptable, I take it home with me, and it becomes an "inside cat" and part of the family.

One night, Ginny and I were taking our nightly walk and happened to go past the same construction site where two months earlier we'd found Topsy. The building was still undergoing extensive renovation. Again Ginny began to whimper, and when I dropped her leash she ran like the wind straight up to the second floor, with me right behind her. But there was nothing to be seen or heard. She must have made a mistake, or maybe she was imagining things.

"Come on, Ginny, let's go," I said. "You won't find anything here."

At which point Ginny approached a pipe that was seven feet long and five inches wide and looked hard at it. She stared at the pipe, looked back at me, then at the pipe, and then at me. Finally, she banged on the pipe with her two front paws until she managed to knock it over.

There, at the bottom of the pipe, was a litter of five kittens no more than a week old. Their eyes were still shut and their little ears were still folded down, that's how young they were. Somebody had thrown them into that pipe like garbage, and left them there to die. I will never compre-

hend how Ginny knew that they were in there by just walking past the building. Even the sharpest dog ears couldn't have heard those tiny, faint, desperate mews. But Ginny has that special gift, a radar of the heart.

As soon as I laid eyes on those five tiny helpless kittens, my eyes were opened; a sudden rush of affection simply poured out of my soul. I just went overboard. I think that's the moment when I fell in love with all cats everywhere, not just the few I had at home. That was the split second in time when Philip Gonzalez became a full-fledged cat lover. And I think that this was the defining moment for Sheilah Harris, too.

From the very first time that Ginny had run into that vacant lot and touched noses with that first homeless cat—the long-haired golden kitten I named Clytemnestra—I believed in my innermost soul that Ginny was possessed of a miraculous kind of sixth sense. But her near-impossible discovery of these wretched abandoned kittens was the most dramatic evidence I had been given. Here was real proof that Ginny could sense—in ways humans and other dogs could not—pain, misery, fear, illness, injury, or disability in helpless cats, and move directly toward it to help. I don't fully understand Ginny's power, but I believe in it completely, and so does everyone who has seen what Ginny has done and can do.

The five newborn kittens were simply loaded with fleas and ticks; they were literally being chewed up alive. I rushed them to the doctor, but the vet had no room to keep them; every one of his cages was full. And they had no nursing bottles for them. So back they came to my house, where I fed them KMR milk, a kitten formula, out of tiny bottles, while Ginny groomed them to get rid of their para-sitical hitchhikers.

I could never have handled those kittens by myself with only one workable hand. Thank heaven for my best friend, Sheilah Harris. She mixed the formula and held the kittens up one by one for me to feed. As for Ginny, she never left their side, and she watched every movement we made with those kittens just like a mother cat would, half-trusting, half-suspicious. Very obviously, she was supervising us. I think Ginny's constant presence was comforting to those tiny scraps of life.

Saving the lives of those kittens, and seeing how tender Ginny was with them, feeding them and handling them her-self, made Sheilah Harris a convert once and for all. Over the months since Ginny had come to live with me, Sheilah had begun to lose her fear of cats and to stop loathing them. But she hadn't yet reached the point of actually loving cats, not until Ginny rescued that litter of five. After that, she was as enthusiastic about cat rescue and about cat feeding as I was myself, as enthusiastic as even Ginny could wish.

It took about four days to get them cleaned up, but miraculously, they all survived and grew. I named them Tiger, Spot, Caesar, Pinky, and Princess. Three months later Pinky and Princess found homes, but as for Tiger, Spot, and Caesar—well, yes, they're still an important part of our fam-ily. I wouldn't think of getting them adopted now.

I got Sheba from a friend of one of my friends, who was moving away and couldn't take her cat with her. My friend put in an impassioned plea for her, and I couldn't resist, not being able to stand the thought of Sheba being placed in an animal shelter after being in her own home for years. So I opened my heart and my front door, and Sheba, a big tiger-striped Manx cat, with only a stub of a tail, strolled in. Right away she made herself at home, deciding that her sleeping place would be in my own bed.

I took Sheba to the vet to have her spayed. The day after I left her there, the doctor's office phoned.

"Mr. Gonzalez? We're calling about that cat you left with us yesterday."

"Sheba?"

"Well, yes, if you can call him that."

"Him?"

"This is not a female, Mr. Gonzalez. This is an altered male. Didn't you know?"

"They told me it was female," I said lamely, feeling very embarrassed.

"Well, he's in good shape, and he certainly doesn't need to be spayed. We'll give him his booster shots, and you can pick him up today. Should we change his name for our records?"

"Yes, please. His new name is Solomon."

Someone I know has an even funnier story to tell. She used to live in a big old farmhouse, and a large striped cat kept coming up on her porch to be fed. One day he asked to be let inside, and soon he was her pet. She named him Camus, and she took him to the vet's and had him neutered.

A few months later, Camus disappeared. He just went out the cat door one morning and didn't come back. She went ballistic. She phoned the local radio station and had his description sent out over the air, although a tiger-striped cat in the country is as common as ragweed. She put out an appeal on the CB radio. She notified the county sheriff and the local humane society. She put posters up. She even offered a generous reward. But there was no sign of Camus. Months later he still hadn't turned up.

A few weeks after she had given up hope, a striped cat came in through the pet entrance cut into the kitchen door. Camus! *Thank you, God.* She grabbed him up and kissed him and hugged him, and he seemed very pleased to see her, too. Then she noticed a strange thing. Camus was still . . . very much male. Noticeably male. She rushed him to the vet, who examined him. No two ways about it. Camus still had possession of his masculine appendages.

"But I thought you neutered him," my friend complained.

The veterinarian looked her straight in the eye. "They grew back," he said simply, and neutered him again.

A couple of months later, the *real* Camus waltzed in through the pet door. Now my friend has two neutered striped male cats, both called Camus. When she told me this story, I shook my head in disbelief. "*'They grew back'?*" What kind of veterinarian was this? What I didn't say out loud was, what kind of pet owner can't tell her own striped cat from a stranger? Every cat in the world has some special something that sets it apart from all the others.

What sets my Solomon apart from my other cats is that he talks.

Almost all cats talk. And they have different, recognizable voices, from the highest-pitched silvery soprano mew to the golden-throated contralto to the creaking "eh eh" that sounds like a hinge that needs oiling. But they almost all talk selectively, when they have something special to say, like "I want to go out" or "Hurry up with those Tender Vittles."

And, if you notice, they almost always talk to humans. With their people, cats can be very conversational. With other cats they tend to use body language rather than vocal speech, especially the position of their ears and tails rather than meows to communicate their feelings. Ears back means they are ready to fight. Ears down means they'd much rather not; please go away if you're feeling aggressive. Ears up and pricked means that something interesting is going on somewhere and in a minute I'll go and investigate. Ears twitching backward usually means a cat has just heard you mentioning his name or the name of his favorite food.

A tail held high in the air like a flag, especially when it's crooked at the tip, is a clear signal to other cats: "I'm feeling fine. Don't bust my chops or break my mood." A tail held low and switching from side to side says plainly, "I'm in a terrible mood. Annoy me at your own risk, because I'm just itching for a fight. And I can take you, buddy."

Not Solomon. Maybe because as a Manx he doesn't have a tail to speak for him, he uses his voice constantly and loudly and to everything and everybody. He never shuts up. If nobody was around he would talk to the paint on the walls. But the funny thing is that he mostly talks to Madame, who can't hear a word he's saying. He gets up in her face and meows and meows and she just ignores him, so he meows some more.

In all those years that I wasted *not* appreciating cats, I used to think that cats were pretty much all alike. I never imagined the many differences among them, the uniqueness of each of their personalities, their whims and preferences, their sweetness and saltiness, their expressiveness. Cats' tails, eyes, ears, noses, whiskers, voices—all tell their own story. Live with a cat and its body language will soon become very clear and easy to understand.

I also didn't think that cats were particularly affectionate. Man, was I wrong! Dogs kiss all the time, but so do cats. When you're stroking a cat on the head, and suddenly her front paw curls around your hand and brings your fingers to her face and she gives them a little, rough lick, well, that's a sensation that nothing can duplicate. When one of my cats curls up on my lap or on my shoulder, he's telling me that there's no place he'd rather be, and no one he'd rather be with, which is an expression of trust and love that overwhelms me with strong feelings I can't even express.

Maybe most cats are not as demonstrative as most dogs, but there are natural reasons for that. Except for lions, all felines are by nature solitary hunters, while dogs form packs. Different behavior patterns have developed in the two species because of that simple natural fact. Dogs think their humans are the top dogs in the pack, and want to please them. Cats are not aloof to their humans, they are just accustomed by nature to pleasing themselves. So when a cat kisses you, it's really flattering and a sure sign of affection, because it's an act of love that pleases the cat to perform.

All this I learned from observing my cats, who are endlessly fascinating to me. Along with my precious Ginny, they've become my family. I can't imagine ever living without a lot of cats again. With Ginny around, needless to say, there's no chance of *that* ever happening.

= 6 =
GINNY AT THE BEACH

GINNY AND I OFTEN take late-night walks on the beach near my home. The ocean beach is quiet and beautiful after dark; even the waves seem a lot more gentle than they are during the day, when they pound the shore. They just seem to roll up on the sand at night. The skies are very clear, and there are more stars twinkling in the heavens than you've ever imagined. Until you've seen the Atlantic Ocean by moonlight, you can't possibly understand how awesome it is; it's overwhelming.

The beach is one of Ginny's favorite places on earth. Something about all that open expanse of sand turns her into a puppy again. As soon as her paws hit the beach, she runs around cheerfully, making figure eights like an ice skater. She dashes forward in a straight line, turns at a right angle, then runs back in a diagonal toward me. Then she wheels around and goes back in the opposite direction, until she has actually traced a figure eight in the sand. She gets rid of a lot of her pent-up energy this way, and you never saw an animal have a better time. But first she always runs toward the ocean, stops to take a good look, then rushes back to me before she gets her feet wet, even though she seems to be fascinated by the ocean and the waves cresting.

Dogs dig; it's an instinct that I'm sure goes back to their most primitive existence, before they were domesticated, when they had to bury their leftover prey so that other hungry dogs wouldn't find it. Ginny really enjoys digging ditches in the sand. Her paws keep moving busily, as though she were doing something of the greatest possible importance. Ginny is very energetic, so her ditches are long and deep. She loves to get down inside them and have me cover her with sand. She wriggles all over with excitement, and then she digs herself out and has me start the game all over again.

One night I saw a jogger on the beach who suddenly just disappeared as though by magic. It turned out he had fallen into one of Ginny's ditches. Fortunately, the sand is soft and he wasn't hurt. I apologized to him, and when he saw

Ginny's little face looking so anxious, he forgave her on the spot.

But after that I was more careful about Ginny's ditches, making sure to fill them in before we left the beach.

I had brought Ginny home from the shelter in March, so when I first began taking her to the beach, it was still cold outdoors, especially at night, and she never ran very far from home base—me. She didn't like getting her feet wet, and the ocean was freezing. But soon the days began to grow longer and the nights became warmer.

One night—it must have been in May—I took Ginny to the beach as usual. Because it was a warm evening in spring, the shoreline was covered with hundreds of little birds darting back and forth on the sand. The tide had come in; the beach was covered with tiny marine creatures that the birds were busy gobbling down. When Ginny saw all the action, she went nuts. She ran toward the shore barking her head off, chasing the birds, as happy as I'd ever seen her. Naturally, the little sandpipers all got out of her way, and I didn't think Ginny was interested in catching any of them, just in chasing them around and making them scatter.

Suddenly, a high wave broke on the shore. For the first time in her life, Ginny was really introduced to the Atlantic Ocean. Salt water came cascading down all over her, drenching her. When the wave receded, there she was, standing in the ocean up to her shoulders. I've never seen anybody look so surprised. Her face said plainly that the wave had tricked her, sneaking up on her from behind. But in a minute or two, as soon as she got used to being wet, Ginny discovered that she enjoyed the Atlantic—it was one more place for her to play.

She began dashing in and out of the breakers, chasing wavelets and little shore birds, but taking care not to get too far away from the shore. After that night, my dog enjoyed the beach even more, playing with the ocean as though it were a favorite toy, but always taking care to stick close to the water's edge. Getting wet all over was not her idea of a good time.

There isn't a dog alive who doesn't get a kick out of a game of Frisbee on the beach, and Ginny Gonzalez is no exception. But remember that Ginny is in large part schnauzer, and the schnauzer breed doesn't like to let go of anything. So I throw the Frisbee with my left hand, and she catches it all right, but then she won't give it back. She hangs on to it tightly with her teeth, growling stubbornly, and I have to wait around doing nothing until she gets bored and drops it. Then I throw it for her one more time, and we go through the same old process again. Between us, we must be playing the longest, slowest game of Frisbee in canine history.

Over the years, the two of us have had quite a few adventures on our nocturnal excursions to the ocean. We usually go late at night, because dogs aren't allowed on the beach; it's a $250 fine if you're caught. Normally, I am a pretty law-abiding guy, but Ginny enjoys the beach so much I don't mind taking the risk for her sake.

She was scampering around on the shore one night,

making her usual figure eights, and I was standing there watching her, when all of a sudden, something hit me hard between the shoulder blades, and I went down like a rock. I must have been knocked out for a minute or two, because when I opened my eyes again, I was lying on my back, and something big and heavy was keeping me pinned down on the sand. Whatever it was, it had the worst breath I ever had the misfortune to be close to. And it was panting and drooling right in my face. It could qualify as anybody's worst nightmare.

As my vision became used to the darkness, I realized that I was trapped under a huge mastiff dog, about one hundred and eighty pounds of solid muscle. It looked, felt, sounded, and smelled like the Hound of the Baskervilles, and I presumed I was done for.

Suddenly, Ginny was racing toward us, barking her head off. I thought it was going to be the end for both of us; the mastiff had me outweighed by about forty pounds, but he outweighed Ginny by at least one hundred and fifty. It was looking bad for the team of Ginny and Gonzalez. In a minute or two, we'd both be kibble.

Then the most astounding thing happened; I couldn't believe my eyes. The mastiff backed down! I don't know what Ginny was saying to him, but she made her point. The huge dog got off me, moved a few feet away, and lay down on his belly with his eyes tightly shut. He actually looked as though he'd been caught with one paw in the cookie jar and was very, very sorry. As for Ginny, she went on yapping at him, sounding exactly like an angry mother scolding a naughty child caught misbehaving, and the mastiff was actually whimpering and flinching. I'd never seen anything so comical as that pair. I had to burst out laughing.

Just then a fellow ran up to us, completely out of breath. It was the mastiff's owner.

"I've been chasing this dog up the beach for two miles," he puffed, and went on to say that he kept his mastiff at home behind a high fence.

"I guess it's not a high enough fence, because tonight my Louie-Louie just jumped over it and ran off to the beach," he added.

I smiled to myself at the mental picture of that huge mastiff sailing through the air to freedom, with his master slogging after him, panting.

When I explained the situation, the guy was totally amazed. He could see for himself who was top dog in this situation, and he was flabbergasted. Ginny was a fraction of the mastiff's size, but she had that huge Louie-Louie pooch eating out of her paw.

"I can't get over it," he marveled. "I never saw him act this way."

The mastiff's owner told me he'd been trying to breed his dog for puppies, but the mastiff had rejected every female brought to him, and none too pleasantly, either. He wouldn't tolerate a girlfriend, no matter how attractive or pedigreed. Now here he was, cringing on his belly in front of a female mixed breed he outweighed four to one. A total wimp-out. Go figure.

Sometimes Ginny and I do venture out onto the beach during the day, risking the fine. We don't go to the more popular sections, where most of the swimmers stay, but keep ourselves to the farther parts that aren't generally sought out by other people. Less sand, more rocks. Whenever we go there during the day, I have to wear welder's goggles, because the medication I still take for my head injuries from the industrial accident makes my eyes sensitive to light.

From time to time I can coax Ginny into the water with me. I used to be a strong swimmer, but these days I can't swim anymore, because I lost 80 percent of the use of my right arm. So all I can do is wade in up to my chest and enjoy the feeling of the ocean on my body. Ginny keeps me company, paddling around close to the shore. She loves me more than she dislikes water, but you can see her heart really isn't into swimming.

She'll grab any excuse to get out of the water, especially if children are playing on the beach. She'll dash ashore, shake the water off her coat, and down she'll go on her belly in the sand, cringing and whimpering as she crawls toward the children, so they won't be afraid of her. If they're friendly, she's in doggy heaven and will let them play with her and stroke her and rub her ears. She'll chase balls and sticks for hours if I let her.

Almost every time we walked the beach we would see homeless dogs, but they usually kept their distance from us. The pathetic animals no longer trust human beings; their experiences have taught them to be wary. Stray dogs haunt the beach. Some of them got lost and were never found; others were put out by their owners to die, because they weren't wanted anymore. Still others were born to the street and had never known a home or human affection.

There was one particular day at the beach I want to tell you about. My friend Sheilah Harris was with us. Ginny was running around, making her usual ice-skater figures, when suddenly we saw three wild dogs racing across the sand toward us. Sheilah gave a loud scream and snatched Ginny up to protect her. Many homeless dogs live on or near the beach, and sometimes they form packs. Some of them are pretty wild, close to savage. They can be scary, and it's best not to run, because they can chase you down and really hurt you. From time to time the beach dogs get rounded up and taken away by the animal authorities, probably to be put permanently to sleep, poor things.

As the dogs came nearer and nearer, I had a sudden memory flashback.

When I was a kid, maybe nine or ten years old, I was walking with some of my friends on the beach, and we saw a pack of homeless dogs. They weren't vicious, just playful, but while we were watching them, the dogcatcher's van pulled up, and the dogcatcher went after them. He nabbed a few of them and shoved them into the back of his van. Then he took off after the others. As soon as he was out of sight, my pals and I went to work. We got the back of the van open, and all the dogs spilled out and ran away—not only the beach dogs, but others he had rounded up, too. We didn't do it to be mischievous; we did it to help the jailed dogs.

Now I was standing there, frozen to the spot, watching these three dogs barking and milling around us, worrying that they might be rabid or vicious, and hoping that they would recognize the grown-up me as one of the good kids who'd set their great-grandfathers and great-grandmothers free that afternoon years ago. Then, from the safety of Sheilah's arms, Ginny began to bark at them.

The dogs stopped cold and barked back, but it wasn't ferocious barking. It sounded almost pleasant, more as if they were all holding a conversation. I could swear that Ginny was asking them if they were hungry, and they were barking back, "Are you serious? Just put down some chow and stand back! We're starving!"

We had no dog food in Sheilah's car, but we had a back seat full of cat food, since we were planning to feed our street cats later that day. To the beach dogs, cat food/dog food was not a fine distinction; it made no difference at all. Eats were eats. They went through twelve large cans of cat food and eight pounds of dry cat chow without stopping for breath. While they were vacuuming their food up, another stray came trotting along and helped them out, just in case they were having trouble choking down all that food by themselves. Ginny stood watching them, and I could swear she was smiling. Whoever is down and out, that's who Ginny always wants most to lend a paw to.

When they'd polished off the last bite, they didn't leave, but hung around with us. Sheilah put Ginny down, and the whole gang of dogs began to play on the beach, digging holes, romping together, pretending that they were dashing into the ocean and, at the last minute, pulling away to run back to us.

It was a day I'll remember for a long time, but there was a sense of sadness hanging over it, too. Out of all the young, healthy dogs on the beach, only one—my Ginny—had a home of her own, a roof over her head, daily food in her belly, and someone to love and love her back. Were those other dogs less deserving? I don't think so. Why shouldn't they, too, have loving homes and humans to protect them? Life can be so cruel and unfair, especially to homeless animals.

From that time on, we always carried dog food as well as cat food with us in the car. It often came in handy. One night, a stray dog came out from under the boardwalk and approached us. He looked as though he was starving, so we got out the food. That dog polished off four cans of dog food and a pound of dry. While he was eating, I got a real good look at him. He seemed to be a fine dog, a German shepherd mix, young and handsome with an intelligent face. I thought that if I could get him to the vet's we might make an adoptable pet out of him and get him a home of his own. I called to him, Ginny called to him, and Sheilah tried to lure him into the car, but he wouldn't come.

The poor stray had large leeches on his ears, but I knew the vet could remove them and make him more comfortable. Still, this pooch was too wary of people to let us take him along with us. He disappeared back under the board-

walk, and although we kept our eyes open for him whenever we went to the beach at night, we never saw him again.

There are cats on the beach, too, and some of them actually go fishing. One night a cat ran past us carrying a fish in its jaws. The fish's tail stuck out on one side of the cat's head, and the fish's head on the other side, just like a Tom and Jerry cartoon. That poor fish was flopping around, trying to get away, but no chance. The cat held on tightly. At least that would be one night the cat had a good meal.

GINNY GETS LOST

Whenever Ginny ran off toward the water, she would always come back to me right away, but on one frightening occasion she didn't. I lost her.

It was a very dark night. The moon was hidden behind thick clouds, and you couldn't see a single star. Ginny ran in the direction of the ocean as usual, but I lost sight of her. She'd already done her figure eights in the sand, letting off a lot of steam, so I expected her to return in a few minutes. But the minutes passed and Ginny didn't come. That was very unlike her.

I called to her. She didn't come. I called to her again. She still didn't come. This was the first time that she ever failed to respond to my voice calling her.

"Ginny!" I yelled. "Ginny!" There wasn't any answer, just the sound of the waves breaking on the shore, and the mewing cries of the seagulls.

This made me uneasy. I walked down to the ocean's edge and along the shoreline, but there was no sign of Ginny. I went out onto the rock jetties, all the way to the end, looking for her on the jetty and—God forbid—in the water. No Ginny. I walked up along the boardwalk. No Ginny, no precious dog galloping back to me.

By now I was pretty panicked. The black sky was moonless, and it was hard to see anything. I didn't know what to do. I thought back to years earlier, to that first time I'd taken Ginny out for a walk at night, when two big dogs came after her and she ran away terrified. She ran all the way home out of fright, and not finding me there, had come back to get me. Or maybe she had come back to rescue me from the big dogs. Knowing Ginny as I did now, I understood that a rescue of her Philip was a real possibility.

Could something have frightened Ginny and sent her running home tonight? If I went home to look there, and she was in trouble somewhere on the beach, I'd be abandoning her. I knew I loved Ginny, but until that moment I didn't realize how much she meant to me, and how important a part of my life she had become. I had to keep looking. So I ducked under the boardwalk and kept searching the dark sand. But there was no little bright-eyed dog down there.

I was frantic with worry; this was totally unlike Ginny, to run off like this and not come back. Something terrible could have happened to her. I began to picture the worst. She might have ventured out into the waves and been pulled under into the freezing ocean. A large wild dog, or a pack of them, might have gotten her, maybe even torn her to pieces. My hands were cold with icy sweat, and I was finding it hard to breathe as these terrible images crowded into my brain.

Then, when I was almost ready to call out the Coast Guard, the Marines, anybody who could help, I heard a single familiar bark. It was coming from the shoreline about two hundred yards up the beach. I ran as fast as I could through the sand, and when I got closer I heard her old familiar whimpering, "Gimme, gimme . . . "

I was so happy to hear her voice I almost burst. But then I thought, Oh, no, she found another cat! Please, Ginny, not another cat!

But it wasn't a cat. When I came up closer I saw a huge shadow emerging from the ocean, out onto the beach. It was too dark to see what kind of creature it was, except that it was a really big one, larger than any dog and certainly larger than a cat. But Ginny wasn't afraid, she kept whimpering and trying to get closer to it. Whatever it was, Ginny wanted to take it home with her . . . with us.

Frankly, I was scared stiff by the huge shadow. I had no idea what it might be; besides, if you're caught walking your dog on the beach, there was that automatic $250 fine, and I was already broke. So I just grabbed the end of Ginny's leash and, against her whimpering protests, grabbed her up and got the hell out of there, without even looking over my shoulder to see if anything was following us. I ran all the way home.

I was so happy to see Ginny again that I didn't even scold her for disappearing on me. But it wasn't until the following day that I found out what happened. I heard over the radio on the local news that a large seal had lost its way and come up on the shore at Long Beach. The seal had been rounded up and taken to an aquarium. The news story mentioned nothing about a little mutt dog finding the seal first and wanting to take it home and keep it as a friend. I had a sudden mental image of being compelled to find the money for large barrels of fresh fish and of never being able to use my bathtub again because Ginny's seal was living in it. I was grateful that I got out of there as fast as I did—without Ginny's seal!

=1=
The Cats of Paradise

I ALWAYS USED TO THINK of Vogue as "the lady of the house," because of all my cats she was the most ladylike and demure. It seemed to me that she must have been accustomed to a home for most of her life, either with a family or maybe in an office (since she loved the telephone and liked to press buttons), before she somehow wound up out on the street. My other inside cats had always been street cats, fighting for survival, scrappy and close to feral. But Vogue wasn't like them; she was a gentle being, with perfect manners and an affectionate heart. She would always sleep in my bed, snuggling up next to me under the covers. Vogue loved Ginny and Ginny loved Vogue, Vogue loved Betty Boop and Betty Boop loved Vogue, but Philip and Vogue had a special bond all their own.

Losing Vogue to inoperable cancer was hard on all of us, especially me, Ginny, and Betty Boop. The day we had to put Vogue mercifully to sleep so that she wouldn't suffer, I thought Betty Boop was going to come apart. She started to cry loudly when she saw Vogue being carried out of my apartment, and after we were gone she didn't stop.

She kept meowing around from room to room, looking everywhere for her friend, poking her nose in all the corners and under the bed. She didn't want to eat, and she hardly closed her eyes to sleep. She would either cry pitifully or just lie there with her chin on her outstretched paws, staring ahead of her without seeing anything. Nothing interested her, and with a lot of cats and a dog in the house, something interesting was always going on. Betty Boop was so sad that I was afraid she would never get over Vogue's passing, and that we might lose her, too. She had never felt the loss of her back feet as sharply as she felt the loss of her best friend.

I got dressed up to the max to take Vogue to the doctor's for her euthanasia. For me, the occasion—a funeral, so to speak—was so solemn that I felt it would only be right and respectful to be wearing a suit and tie. At the doctor's office Vogue clung to me, terrified, and I held her tightly in my arms.

"We're going home, Vogue," I whispered to her. "We're going home." It wasn't exactly a lie. In my heart, I guess, I believed that my cat really was going home, home to her maker. I believed that she was being taken to a place where she would never feel pain or fear again.

The vet put the needle into her leg, and gave her a small shot, just enough medication to relax her and keep her from being afraid. I was still holding her. Nothing would have made me let her go. When she was relaxed, the doctor gave her a full needle, and she went limp in my arms, dying quickly and peacefully without pain or fear.

When I saw the life slipping out of Vogue, I felt the life slipping out of me as well. This was the first time I ever had to put a beloved pet to sleep. It never gets any easier, but I think that the first time is the worst time.

DARLENE

Meanwhile, our rescue work continued on the street. Ginny, Sheilah, and I had targeted an abandoned building occupied by squatters, which also housed a large population of homeless cats. The squatters tolerated the cats, probably because the cats kept the rodent population under control, but they couldn't afford or didn't bother to feed them. That was left up to us, and the three of us went there every day, twice a day. One of the cats especially appealed to me, a large Maine coon cat with thick, long hair and tabby markings. I named her Darlene. In my opinion Darlene was so beautiful that she had an excellent chance of being adopted into a good home if we could just catch her, get her spayed, and have her inoculated.

But Darlene had a mind of her own—and other intentions. She was determined not to be caught, and she managed to avoid us very cleverly for a long time. Then she vanished; we didn't see her for a while, and I was afraid something terrible had happened to her. When she turned up again, looking thin but otherwise not too much the worse for wear, Ginny, Sheilah, and I uttered sighs of relief.

Every time I went over to the squatters' building, I took along a cat carrier. One day Darlene seemed unusually friendly—she actually came over to me while I was feeding the other cats. This looked like my chance to capture her. I quietly opened the carrier. Slowly I reached out to her and began to stroke her gently, and she stayed in one place, letting me touch her for the first time. I was just about to put Darlene into the cat carrier when one of the squatters, who'd been sitting there watching, yelled out to me.

"That's a tomcat! You can't catch a tomcat!"

I almost had her, but when he shouted he spoiled my chance to catch her. Darlene spooked and began to struggle. I had hold of her with my one good hand, and I made a grab for her, but missed. She didn't want to be grabbed, so she got away from me easily and dashed away at top speed around the corner. I followed her.

But it was icy underfoot, and I just couldn't move quickly enough. I had to hold on to the wall with my left hand just to take one small step after another. When I got to the corner, I gasped in horror. There was a large tabby lying dead by the side of the road, the victim of a hit-and-run. I was certain it was Darlene. She had run away from me in panic, without looking where she was going. I must have chased

Darlene into traffic; I was responsible for her death.

I burst into tears of guilt, remorse, and sorrow. If only I hadn't grabbed for her! All I wanted to do was help this pretty creature find a loving home, and now she was lying there dead and I was to blame. I picked the little body up and went to Sheilah's house. The ground was frozen solid, the earth too hard for me to bury her, so Sheilah drove me to the animal shelter, where I arranged and paid for the cat's burial. I still thought the dead cat was Darlene.

But it wasn't Darlene. Because a strange and wonderful thing happened. On the day that Vogue went to sleep forever, I came home from the vet's office and went right out again with Sheilah to feed the squatters' cats. With Vogue's death, homeless animals had become more important to me than ever, because I saw their lives—all life—as even more precious.

Suddenly, Darlene appeared out of nowhere and simply jumped up into Sheilah's arms. It was as though she was saying, "Here I am. I know you thought I was dead, but I'm not. I'm yours now." With full hearts, Sheilah and I drove her over to the doctor's office and the cat remained there for several weeks.

Darlene had a big surprise in store for us. It was impossible for me to tell, under her thick coat of fur, that she was pregnant, but in fact she was *very* pregnant. In fact, the night after we took her away from the squatters, she gave birth to a litter of kittens at the vet's.

Somehow I had the feeling that Darlene had been purposely sent to us to take Vogue's place. Otherwise, why had she turned up so mysteriously on the very day that Vogue died? So a few weeks later, when she had recovered from her spaying and her kittens were old enough to be parted from her, instead of turning her back out or looking for someone to adopt her, I brought her home. I also brought home one of Darlene's kittens, a little gray beauty named Sasha, who grew up to be very talkative and extremely intelligent.

Betty Boop was still in deep mourning for Vogue, missing meals and remaining indifferent to life. But as soon as I opened the carrier and set Darlene down on the living-room floor, Betty Boop perked up. She rabbit-hopped right up to her to make friends. She sniffed at Darlene, and then she licked her on the cheek, in that sweet way that cats have when they are saying hello. Darlene responded, and they became best friends on the spot. They still are the closest pals. As though it was meant to be, Betty Boop accepted Darlene as Vogue's replacement. She went back to eating regularly, and as for Darlene—well, today she weighs a tubby twenty-one pounds. I was now back up to nine cats.

But my tenth wasn't far away. One of the street cats, a very pretty calico, was wearing a collar but no ID tag, so I thought she might be lost and a grieving family might be searching for her. I asked all around the neighborhood, I even put up posters describing her, but nobody came forward to claim her. So I popped her into a carrier and took her to the vet's, where I left her for adoption. Every time I visited the vet's, which was practically every day, I would see her there, waiting for a home, but nobody offered her one. She was just too pretty and sweet to leave in a cage, so I took her home and named her Calliope after her calico fur.

VENUS

Remember the construction site where Ginny found Topsy, the tiny kitten born with hypoplasia cerebella? It was a large building undergoing renovations. At one time it was the location of the Paradise Nursing Home, and I still thought of it as the Paradise. As the construction continued, the former old-age-home site became a gathering place and shelter for a number of homeless cats, so Ginny and I visited it every day with cans of food and fresh water.

There were about forty homeless cats at the site I still called Paradise, and four of them ran around together. I named them Venus, Lulu, Penelope, and Hector. I used to call them the Big Four. Along with the other three dozen cats, Ginny and I fed them twice a day. Lulu, Penelope, and Hector were long-haired cats. There were a large number of homeless long-hairs in the neighborhood, and I always thought that they had all descended from Clytemnestra, that little red long-haired kitten who was the first homeless cat to touch noses with Ginny soon after I got her. I also used to think that, if I had taken that red kitten home and gotten her spayed, it would have kept the cat population down. But in those days I didn't care all that much for cats; my deep affection for them would develop later, as Ginny introduced me to loving them. So how could I have known?

Venus was a short-haired tabby, so she probably didn't come from the same litter as the three others, who looked like littermates. One day she turned up missing, just disappeared off the surface of the earth. Had she been hit by a car? It was entirely probable, because automobiles are the most frequent killers of cats.

When Venus had been gone for about a week, Ginny pulled at her leash until I let her lead me up to a garage in the neighborhood. And there was Venus, sitting in the window, looking thin and pitiful. There was only a screen on the garage window, because it was summertime, and I removed it.

We learned later that the garage was infested with mice, so the people who owned the house had probably gone to Paradise and picked out Venus to hunt them. They locked her up in the garage without food, thinking that if they fed her she wouldn't go after mice, but if she caught them, she could eat them.

Venus was used to our good food twice a day, and she turned up her nose at mice. So she was literally starving to death and couldn't get out until Ginny found her.

Venus and Ginny were very obviously pleased to see each other. After Ginny had groomed the cat's fur with her tongue and teeth, Venus ran off to Paradise, and lived there happily for the next couple of months.

Then she disappeared again. One more time, Ginny led me in the direction of the garage and, sure enough, Venus was back inside, kept a prisoner behind locked doors. For the second time I removed the screen and we liberated her and returned her to Paradise. Ginny had rescued her twice.

When Venus was missing for the third time, Ginny and I didn't waste a minute, but headed straight for the garage. But this time she wasn't there, and we couldn't find her anywhere. She didn't show up for four months, but when she did, she looked terrific and was in fine shape. Her whereabouts were a mystery we never solved, but she soon took off again for a while. Now Venus comes and goes, and because she's always in such good condition when we see her I have the theory that she found herself a home, and just comes back every now and then to visit her old Paradise friends and Ginny.

As of this writing, I haven't seen Venus for seven months, but I like to picture her sitting on a lap in a pleasant room, warm and well fed, purring away happily while kindly hands stroke her fur.

DOTTY AND DITTO

Ginny once found two cats living in a junkyard. She literally dragged me to the yard by her leash, and all I could do was follow. By now I knew for certain that a cat or cats needed rescue or else Ginny wouldn't be so determined. And of course there *were* cats in trouble in that junkyard. The junkyard owner let the cats live there, but he didn't exactly feed them. I say "exactly," because he kept eight live chickens, and he fed his chickens only table scraps—anything left over, or anything he could scrounge from neighborhood restaurants and other people's tables. If the cats were lucky, they could grab a few scraps before the chickens got to them, but those were pretty aggressive, street-smart chickens, and they'd peck at the cats and drive them away from the food. The poor pusses were no match for those angry, dog-in-the-manger birds.

When Ginny found the two cats I decided to call them Dotty and Ditto—after the cute twin children in Bil Keane's comic strip "The Family Circus." The cats were in pretty bad shape and close to starvation. Dotty had been pecked everywhere on her body by those territorial chickens and she had open sores all over her. Ditto had a bad leg—it was swollen and infected—and he was limping around on three feet. I thought he was a black cat because he was so afraid of everything that he would come out only after nightfall and in the dark he appeared to be almost featureless and colorless. Which is why I thought of him as "Ditto."

Even though he limped, Ditto was surprisingly fast. He was impossible to catch and so was Dotty. But I was bound and determined to get hold of them and get them out of that junkyard, because both of them were badly in need of immediate medical treatment.

One day, Dotty fell desperately ill. She must have eaten bad food; the junkyard food was often old, stale, and rancid. Or perhaps somebody tried to poison her, because she was close to death by the time I found her and got her to the vet's. She was there about two weeks, recovering her health and strength, then she was returned to the street, all well and spayed and inoculated.

The next thing I knew, Dotty was very sick again. She was out on the street only a short while before something she ate almost killed her a second time. This time I was pretty sure somebody was setting out poison, but I didn't know who. I scooped Dotty up and rushed her to the doctor's, swearing to myself and to her that if she got well, she would be coming home with me, and nobody would ever get the chance to poison her again. And that's what happened; Dotty lived to become Gonzalez cat number eleven.

I was still having a lot of trouble getting hold of Ditto, and from the little I could see when I put his food out every night, his leg didn't seem to be getting any better. I knew I had to get him to the doctor before the infection killed him. One of my new cat-loving friends, Ramona, owned a humane trap called a Tomahawk, which doesn't catch an animal's tail or paw when it slams shut, so she set it out in the junkyard. She baited it with food, and Ditto hobbled straight into it. We finally had him.

The vet told me that Ditto's leg was in pretty bad condition; it was terribly swollen and infected.

"I might have to take it off," he told me.

"No! Absolutely not! No amputation!" I remembered what had happened to my own arm and how I'd had to fight the doctors to keep it. How could I do any less for this helpless animal?

At that time, I had no thought of adopting Ditto myself, but when I came back the following day to check on him, I saw him cleaned up and in the light for the first time. He wasn't black at all, he was a sweet-faced tabby with beautiful markings, and I simply fell in love with him. There were no two ways about it. Whether Ditto came through this ordeal with three legs or four, he was going to be my cat from then on. And he was too much his own cat to be called merely Ditto, so when I got him home—he came out of the cat carrier on all four legs—I renamed him Napoleon, after my collection of military memorabilia, and especially after myself, because my army buddies had nicknamed me—a little guy—Napoleon.

PARADISE

The security guard at Paradise was a kindly man, and he hated cruelty to animals. So he let Ginny and me through the fence twice a day to feed our cats. But eventually that situation had to come to an end.

"The owners of this place don't want these cats around anymore," the guard warned us one night. "I don't know how they're planning to do it, maybe by putting down poisoned food, but there's talk of exterminating them. If you want those cats to survive, you'd better move them out of here."

That was more easily said than done. Sheilah and I became very depressed when we sat down and tried to figure out how to empty out Paradise. Although we knew the cats living there well, and had names for them, some of them were always wandering off, while new cats wandered in all the time. How could we be sure we had all of them? It looked like a monumental job, more than we could handle, yet we knew we had to get as many cats as possible away from there before the owners of the building took steps to destroy them. The time pressure added greatly to our stress.

The cat roundup was one of the most difficult things that Ginny and Sheilah and I had done, and it took us several days. We began to catch them and carry them out one by one, with me having the use of only my left arm. We didn't know much about traps then (we hadn't yet met Ramona), except that the so-called "humane" traps would sometimes slam down on a cat's head, or catch a cat's leg or tail and break it. So we rejected those, instead putting the cats, one at a time as we could get hold of them, into cat carriers. And during the rescue operation I was still looking for a safe place to relocate them.

Sheilah had been feeding cats on the street, driving around in her Nova to places Ginny and I couldn't reach on foot. One day she saw an elderly woman feeding cats out of the trunk of her car. The trunk was filled with cat food, just like Sheilah's. So of course she stopped for a talk, Cat Lady to Cat Lady. That's how we met Ramona, who would go around not only feeding strays but catching them in her special trap, the Tomahawk. The difference between Ramona and us was that Sheilah and I tried to find homes for the cats we trapped, and Ramona couldn't bear to let any of the cats go. She would bring them all to her house and make them part of her family. She had one hundred and forty cats!

She showed Sheilah how the Tomahawk worked, and it was impressive—efficient and safe. Then she offered to help us clean out Paradise. We accepted, and Ramona's traps became a godsend to us. After that, we were able to get all the cats to safety in record time, and Ramona became a good friend (it was she who managed to trap Ditto/Napoleon).

By the time that Dotty came to live with us, Ginny and I were feeding about twenty-six outside cats. During the cold winter months, I was as much concerned with keeping the outside cats from freezing as with keeping them from starving. What Sheilah and I did was this: we collected a number of cardboard grocery cartons to use as shelters, wrapping them in heavy plastic outside and inside to keep the cold out. We lined them with anything we could get our hands on—towels, old blankets, a couple of old coats, even a castoff down coat—whatever would help our outside cats find some protection from the brutally cold weather.

We put those cartons into a vacant lot across the street from Paradise and brought the evicted cats there, together with fresh food and water to tempt them to stay. It was kind of a pussycat shantytown that we built, surrounded by junked automobiles, rusting stoves, refrigerators without doors, and other twentieth-century discards, but it did provide some decent shelter from the cold, and the homeless cats accepted the cartons gratefully, spending their nights there. The place became, in my mind, Paradise Two.

JASMINE

When Ginny and I adopted Topsy, we added all her sisters and brothers and cousins to our twice-a-day catering route. Although the cats and kittens were fearful of me at first, they soon became used to me, and I named them all. Jasmine was born into the same litter that Topsy came from; she was Topsy's sister. She was one of the outside cats we were feeding, so when she didn't turn up for about four days I became pretty worried. It's true that homeless cats sometimes choose to move on, but this was wintertime and

Jasmine was getting fed twice a day. I didn't believe that she would take off on her own and leave her regular meals.

From time to time one of the outside cats would be missing and never be seen again. What I strongly suspected was that some really evil cat-poisoner was at work, considering what had happened to Dotty. That's still my opinion, although the terrible thought gives me chills. I don't know what I'd do if I had proof that someone was out to kill these helpless cats, but I wouldn't be responsible for my own actions, because I know I'd lose control when I met up with him or her.

I was being eaten up by worry. Could Jasmine have been poisoned? Could she be lying dead somewhere? Or, even worse, dying slowly in agony? I lost several nights of sleep agonizing over these questions.

On the fourth day after Jasmine disappeared, when it was time to go home, Ginny didn't want to leave Paradise Two, the vacant lot. I tugged at her leash, but she wouldn't obey. Instead, she kept pulling me over to one of the plastic-covered cartons. When I let go of her leash, Ginny began to nose at it, trying to turn the big box over with her snout.

"Come on, Ginny! Let's go! There's nothing in there."

But Ginny wouldn't leave that carton alone. She kept shoving at it with her nose, tipping it, and obviously trying to push it over. I came up close to her and looked inside, but to me the box appeared totally empty.

"Don't be so stubborn. Come on, Ginny! It's cold out here! Let's get home before I freeze!"

But Ginny wasn't paying any attention to me. All her attention was focused on that cardboard box, and her entire body was quivering with excitement. Her tail thumped again and again, a sure sign that something was up with Ginny. She gave the carton one more push, and it fell over. Now that it was up-ended, you could see into it. Again I looked inside, and I could just barely make out something huddled in the far corner of the box. It didn't look like a cat at first, because it was covered all over with some slimy substance and you couldn't make out any features. The figure turned out to be Jasmine, badly hurt. She was oozing infection from her open wounds, and her fur was all matted down and wet with the infected matter.

I couldn't imagine what had happened to poor little Jasmine. Had she been in a fight? But these were more dreadful wounds than any she could have gotten in a simple catfight. Unless a lot of cats or dogs had ganged up on her all at once. Her wounds bore all the signs of a brutal, savage attack. Jasmine had been a target—and a victim. I had never seen a cat in such terrible condition. It broke my heart just to look at her, she was suffering so much. If Ginny hadn't insisted on finding her right then, Jasmine wouldn't have had the smallest chance at life. As it was, she probably wasn't going to make it, or so the vet told me. In addition to exposure and starvation, she was suffering from a major infection running all through her bloodstream.

"Do anything you can to save her," I begged him. "Anything."

Jasmine was so far gone it took six weeks in the hospital to bring her back to life. If cats do have nine lives, as the legend says, I'm sure she was robbed of at least five of them. But there's a happy ending to this little cat's story. When she left the vet's she went directly to Sheilah's apartment to live, and she's still there, completely cured, well and cheerful, and enjoying a good life and the love of everybody, surrounded by dog, cat, and human friends.

While we were feeding the cats not far from Paradise, at the squatters' tenement where we'd found Darlene, there was another cat who ran around with her, and I named this cat Rosie. Actually, there were a lot of cats there, and I had names for them all.

"They're going to throw the squatters out and board that place up so that nothing can get inside," my friend the security guard told me. "You've got about two days to get those cats out safely before the building owners get rid of them."

Sheilah and I, helped by Ginny of course, did another roundup. We picked up Graybeard, Friday, Streaky, and the Chairman, got them all inoculated and neutered, and moved them to Paradise Two. But, although we looked high and low, we couldn't find Rosie anywhere.

The winter of 1993 was a terribly cold one, with a lot of snow and ice. Wherever Ginny and I walked, we kept an eye out for Rosie, but I wasn't at all convinced we'd find her. In winter, the cards are really stacked against a homeless cat, and my heart told me sadly that Rosie was probably gone for good and that we'd never see her again. In weather like this, without food or shelter, how could a helpless little animal possibly survive?

One night, after a particularly severe ice storm, Ginny and I were out for our late walk, when she ran directly to a Dumpster on our route. Behind the Dumpster was a cardboard box, and Ginny made a beeline for it, making her familiar whimpering noises. Using her paws and nose, she turned the box over and barked once, a signal to me. Slipping and sliding on the ice, I hurried over to look.

There was something in the box. All I could see were two huge eyes staring at me. No cat, just eyes.

It was Rosie, but she was so emaciated and weak I could see her practically dying right there in front of me. I rushed home to get Sheilah and her Chevy Nova, and we drove little Rosie to the vet's. We drove very slowly, no more than twenty miles an hour, not only because the roads were icy, but because we were afraid that if the car went over any bumps in the road it would bump the remaining breath right out of Rosie. That's how close to the brink she was. I held her starved and frozen little body in my lap, warmly wrapped in my jacket, and I prayed to God to spare her life.

Why did you send Ginny to find her if she wasn't meant to live? I asked God.

She did live. Thanks to God and Ginny, Rosie became one more cat who came back from the brink of death and moved in with us to stay. Rosie became my thirteenth cat, so I think that thirteen must be a very lucky number. At least it was for Rosie.

As for Friday, he used to follow me all the time, like a little shadow. Until one day when he met a beautiful blonde, and he followed her instead. Smart cat. The lady took to him and brought him home with her. She didn't keep him, though, because the blonde's boyfriend really took a shine to Friday, and gave him an even better home. Now Friday is living off the fat of the land.

The Chairman doesn't want to be a house pet. He loves

his freewheeling life on the street, so I go on feeding him, and when the weather gets too cold for him he comes up on my terrace. Outside my apartment, I keep a number of cat carriers with their doors open on a small terrace. Inside the carriers, I put warm, comfortable things like lamb fleece or old towels for the cats to lie on. On cold nights, my "outside" cats know where they can flop for the night. They know they'll be sheltered and yet still be free to come and go as they please. It's an arrangement that suits their independence. On really bitter nights, I bring the carriers, cats and all, inside my apartment to get warm, but I lock the little carrier doors so that the street cats can't bring any potential infections to my "inside" cats.

=8=
LITTLE BLIND JACKIE

SCARLETT LIVED IN PARADISE TWO and was pregnant with a litter of kittens. I tried hard to catch her before she gave birth, but it wasn't possible. She was very self-protective, as pregnant cats often are, and it made her suspicious and elusive. Then one day I noticed that Scarlett was skinny again. She had given birth, but she successfully hid her litter away. Cats are clever that way; when it comes to protecting their babies no animal is smarter or braver than a cat. So for several weeks I couldn't find the kittens. I would feed Scarlett extra-large portions of food because she was a nursing mother, and I knew that the kittens were doing well on her milk.

Even so, I was anxious about that litter. I didn't know how well their mother was able to protect them from their natural enemies: big rats, other cats—especially males, who are frequently deadly to kittens who aren't of their own making—and, especially, to protect them from ill-meaning people. As it turned out, I was right to worry.

When I figured the kittens to be about seven weeks old, I made up my mind to get hold of them. Kittens were a lot easier to find homes for than full-grown cats. Naturally, the first one I turned to for help was Ginny.

"Ginny, find those kittens," I ordered, and off she ran across the lot, past the junked automobiles and all the other trash. She trotted straight up to an old car door and began her cat-whimpering. The door was hollow, and there was a big hole in the steel. I did a very foolish thing; I stuck my one good hand in there without knowing what it might meet. There might be rats hiding in there, and I might have been bitten and infected. But I struck it lucky; my fingers touched fur. Good old Ginny had located the kittens' hiding place.

All at once, the babies broke cover and scattered in all directions. There seemed to be four or five of them, but I could only catch one. I held her up and looked at her in surprise. She was a pretty little Siamese, blue eyes, buff-colored fur, chocolate ears and paws and tail and all. Scarlett was not Siamese, so the kitten couldn't possibly have come from her litter. I'd seen Siamese cats hanging around Paradise from time to time, so some pregnant Siamese female must have dropped her litter there. One of the kittens who'd escaped seemed also to be Siamese, from what little I could see of it as it scuttled away. This little girl in my hand was such a glorious kitten I named her Gloria on the spot.

I didn't realize it, but a woman was watching me from across the street, from her window in the apartment building that overlooked Paradise Two. She had been looking at me for a long time through a pair of binoculars, and now she left a note for me at my home.

"I saw you catch a baby Siamese and I'm interested in that cat. Will you please call me?" I looked her up, and recognized her as the owner of a beautiful Dalmatian dog. I'd seen her many times walking that dog, and I knew him by name and reputation. He was the sworn enemy of all the cats in the neighborhood.

"I can't give you little Gloria. Dodger hates cats," I reminded her. "He'd have that kitten for breakfast."

"It's not for me, it's for my sister. She had a Siamese cat for a long time. The cat died recently and my sister is all broken up over it. I want to give her that kitten."

I shook my head. "That's crazy. You can't just substitute one cat for another. It doesn't work that way. What if someone's mother died. Would you say, 'Here, here's a nice old lady to take her place'?" But the woman was insistent. She begged and pleaded for Gloria, and finally I gave in, under the condition that if her sister didn't want her, Gloria would come right back to me.

At first, the woman's sister wouldn't hear of it. No, no, no! She didn't even want to lay eyes on Gloria. She had loved her old cat so much that even the thought of replacing her was more than she could deal with. But then she saw Gloria, a cute, tiny, irresistible bundle of fur with the same markings as her late pet. It was love at first sight between human and cat. She hugged and kissed that kitten until she almost rubbed its chocolate markings off.

So Gloria found an immediate home. I never saw the other Siamese kitten again. Gloria was lucky, but two of the other three kittens in her foster mother Scarlett's litter—whom I named Anything, Tulip, and Petunia—were not so fortunate as Gloria.

I thought at first that Petunia was male, so I named him Paris after the prince of Troy who fell in love with Helen of Sparta, stole her from her husband the king, and started the Trojan War. But Paris, a cunning little tiger-stripe, soon proved to be female, was rechristened with a more appropriate name, and I was successful in placing her in a good home.

I had high hopes for Scarlett's three other kittens, but when Ginny and I got to Paradise Two one day, I went into shock. Those two babies had been beaten without mercy and were in terrible condition. Tulip had a broken leg, and one of her ears was missing. Little Anything was beaten so badly that he was mangled and could barely crawl, but he did crawl up to me begging me for help. I tried to get Tulip, too, but she was hard to catch. Yet, as soon as I put down the Tomahawk trap, Tulip limped into it. Around the wound left by her missing ear, maggots were crawling. The pathetic sight of these two tiny abused innocents made me feel ill.

I didn't have time to fetch Sheilah and her car; I grabbed

a taxi and Ginny and I took the two little victims to the vet's. As badly off as Tulip was, she could still be saved, but poor little Anything died right there, at the vet's, in front of our horrified eyes.

Who was the monster who could have inflicted such damage and pain on a pair of helpless kittens? I was so choked with rage I was determined to find out.

A couple of days later, I saw Scarlett at Paradise Two, batting something shiny around with her paw. I picked it up; it was a dog's identification tag. I asked around, and I was told that the owner of the dog lived nearby, and witnesses assured me that this was the man who had beaten the kittens. And he'd used a metal chain!

I went out looking for him, and when I found him at last I confronted this guy. I'm five feet six and a half inches tall and he was about six foot two, but that didn't matter to me. I was so angry I couldn't see straight, and I was ready to tear him apart with my one good hand.

"Did you beat those cats with a chain?!"

"Yeah, so what? What's it to you? They got germs, those damn cats. I didn't want them to give my dog germs."

I saw red. I was eager to take him on, even if he was a head taller than me. "You beat those cats, and I'm gonna kill you, buddy!" I roared and went straight at him. Two people had to pull me back and hold me, and the slimy rat beat a fast retreat.

When he sees me on the same side of the street today, that guy crosses over and looks the other way. If he'd known that I only had the use of one arm, I doubt he would have been so intimidated. But like all bullies he's a coward, and I know he'll think twice about beating up on a defenseless cat while I'm still around to get up in his face.

One day in 1993 I was chasing a cat in front of the squatters' building, trying to get it into a carrier, when my leg suddenly turned on me and bent the wrong way. I went down like a brick wall under the wreckers' ball. I could barely manage to stand up, and when I did, my knee was killing me. I tried to ignore it, and I just went on with my rescue work, but a month after the accident my knee was still out of whack and hurt a lot, so I took myself to an orthopedic surgeon.

"You've torn the ligaments in your knee," he told me. "It looks like you may have injured it originally in your industrial accident, weakened it, and now reinjured it. I'm going to have to operate, and afterward bandage it up, and you're going to have to stay off that leg for weeks. No cat feeding for a while. That's an order."

So I was back in the hospital again, to undergo more surgery. After I got out of the hospital I had to stay on my back for a couple of weeks, out of commission. There were only two bright spots in having to stay home. One was knowing that Sheilah was carrying on the good work. She took Ginny out with her several times a day, and the two of them went cat feeding. The other bright spot was that I got to stay home with my houseful of cats. They were wonderful company for me and seemed to be glad to have me around. The only thing was that they wouldn't let me read. As soon as I picked up a book, a newspaper, or a magazine, they would crowd around me and grab at the pages with their paws, pushing whatever I was reading right out of my hands, and

even tearing holes in the paper. They made it plain that they were expecting my complete and undivided attention.

The cats enjoyed television, though. Whenever I turned on the TV, they would all join me on the sofa. As many as could fit on my lap settled down there, some sat next to me, a few perched on my shoulders, and one—Napoleon—actually stretched out on my knee bandage. Not only did they appreciate the closeness to me, but they liked watching the movement on the screen.

Darlene would sometimes sit on the floor right in front of the set, and tap her paw on the TV screen, trying to catch the moving wheel on "Wheel of Fortune." They especially liked the sound of bird song from nature programs and would snap to attention whenever they heard the chirping. Their whiskers would bristle and their ears stand straight up, and they would crane their heads forward. Some of them would growl in their throats, like the instinctive hunters cats are, as though they couldn't wait to get their paws on those birds. Many times I'd have to turn the volume on the set up high, because I couldn't hear anything over the sound of a dozen cats purring at once.

But as much fun as it was to share my day with my cats, I was glad when the doctor said I could resume my normal activities. I was still hurting and bandaged when I hobbled down to Paradise Two, where Sheilah was out feeding. But I was happy to be there anyway.

"I've got a surprise for you." She grinned when she saw me coming. "Look!"

My mouth dropped open in astonishment. There, where we had put up a shantytown of cardboard carton shelters, stood a neat little wooden house with entrance and exit doors. I could see cats going in and out.

"It's warm and it's weatherproof," added Sheilah. "The cats love it."

She told me that a couple—husband and wife—who lived across from the lot in an apartment building, had built the shelter for the cats of Paradise Two. What a generous thing for them to have done! The wooden shelter stayed there for a while, until the owner of the lot said the house had to go. He claimed that he got a lot of complaints that the cats were bringing rodents. Which was just nuts, because cats get rid of rodents, they don't attract them.

So the friendly couple moved the house to another location, where it now shelters other cats. And Ginny, Sheilah, and I had to relocate our outside cats as well. Near my house is a strip of concrete dividing two-way traffic, one-way on either side of the concrete. Three trees grow on it, and cats were beginning to congregate there. I wouldn't have chosen a place in the middle of traffic to feed cats, but the cats themselves chose it for me. I started feeding them at the middle tree. So that feeding tree became a stop in my regular daily routine.

Paradise Two is home base to only about four cats now. There's Van Gogh—no, she has *two* ears, but to me she looks like a Van Gogh painting—Ghost, Hector, and Herod. We also feed cats at Miller Street. Miller Street was one of Ramona's feeding stations. She had been feeding four or five cats there every day, but a man who hated cats threatened her and actually pushed her, although she's frail and about seventy-five years old. I told her not to feed the cats there anymore, that I would take over. I'd like to see any-body try to push me, and if I'd been around the day he pushed Ramona it would have been curtains for him.

One day I saw him with my own eyes roughly shooing the cats away, and I confronted him.

"Why don't you leave these cats alone?" I demanded. "They're not hurting you. They're not hurting anybody."

"I hate them, I wish they were all dead," he spat at me. "I'd like to kill them myself."

"If you lift one finger against one of these cats, if you damage so much as a whisker, I'll fix you good," I growled, and I meant every word. After that, the guy kept himself out of my way; he wouldn't take me on. Helpless elderly ladies were more his speed.

One day Ginny pulled me over to Andy, a white-bellied tiger, about four months old, who was out walking the streets. He was a really friendly animal, and he played with Ginny enthusiastically. I grabbed him up and carried him to the vet to be neutered. The next day a local man went to the office to find a small kitten for his sister, who had moved to Pennsylvania. He saw Andy, and even though Andy wasn't strictly a tiny kitten, being a long-legged adolescent, the man was smitten on the spot. The vet's office called me up. "Did you want to have this cat adopted?"

"If it's going to a good home."

"There's somebody here who seems really reliable, and he's willing to pay for Andy's shots and neutering."

That had never happened to me before, and it has never happened to me again, but it was terrific. Andy found a new life and a good home right away and it didn't cost me a cent. He's living happily in Pennsylvania now, with a family of his own.

Freya, named for a very good friend of mine, was a cat at Miller Street we started feeding. Sheilah liked Freya, and thought she'd make somebody a great pet if we could only catch her. She was a large female, about eighteen pounds of her, and when we set out the trap she was too big for it—the entrance to the trap wouldn't go down.

That same night Freya gave birth to four kittens, and we were able to bring all five to the vet. A woman looking for a companion for her cat saw Freya at the vet's office and fell in love with her. Then her four babies were adopted as soon as they were old enough. That was a great cat rescue in my book—five for the price of one.

JACKIE

Jackie was a small black kitten our vet was holding for adoption. She was sweet and affectionate. As soon as Ginny laid eyes on her, she started her "Hallelujah Chorus" of "Gimme that cat ... please ... please." Which meant, of course, that this kitten had a disability. She was totally blind in both eyes.

"No, Ginny, you can't have her," I told her. "We're going to take Jackie to Pet Expo."

Long Island Pet Expo 1993 was a joint venture of a group of local animal shelters, together with the Humane Society, other animal rescue groups, and even pet shop concessionaires. It was held at a large, centrally located place, the Nassau Coliseum, where the public was invited in to adopt homeless animals. The shelters brought in cats and dogs and other pets so that people could actually take home a new friend.

The night before we brought Jackie there, Sheilah and I made a video. Sheilah was seen holding the little kitten in her arms, up to her face. Jackie's paws were around Sheilah's neck in a hug, with her back to the camera. Sheilah told the viewers how sweet Jackie was, how loving and cute, and only at the end of the video did she turn the kitten around and tell everybody Jackie was blind. It was very dramatic and effective.

So effective that Jackie never made it into the Expo. Ken, a man who worked for our local Humane Society, was so impressed and touched by Jackie's sweetness and blindness that he snapped her up as company for his one and only cat, Polly, who was named for her extra toes, a common mutation called polydactylism.

Ken gave Jackie a loving home for almost two years, then he died suddenly and unexpectedly of natural causes. New homes had to be found immediately for Jackie and Polly. Ken's sister in California volunteered to take Polly in, but little blind Jackie was more than she was ready to handle. So Jackie was returned to the vet's office to find another home. Here we had one more handicapped cat, and you know by now what that means. Ginny saw her there again, and again she uttered pleading whimpers for her. I gave my dog her way as usual, and now Jackie lives down at Sheilah's apartment. Ginny visits Sheilah's cats every day, and whenever she comes in, Jackie finds her, snuggles up next to her, and goes happily to sleep.

Sheilah and I had a consultation with the vet, who said that an operation on one of her eyes might restore some of Jackie's sight. We decided to go ahead with it. After her surgery in January of 1995, for the first time in her young life Jackie had vision in one eye. Seeing opened up a wonderful new world to her. If you want to see a happy cat, you should watch her chasing her ball around.

And, for the first time since she came to live with us, Jackie can see Ginny.

= 9 =
ANGEL GINNY

A LOT OF PEOPLE THINK I'm out of my mind because almost every cent that comes in goes out immediately toward the feeding and rescuing of cats. Because I never buy anything for myself, out of my workmen's comp I even manage to pay the veterinarian, and those bills can really mount up, even with the generous discount he gives me.

Tulip, who was badly beaten with a chain, cost me between $700 and $800 in medical bills. So did Rosie, who was starved and frozen. Both of those cats had to have three weeks of hospitalization. Van Gogh, who was in the animal hospital for six weeks after surgery for a tipped uterus, ran up a bill of over $1,000. Poor little Jasmine, who was badly wounded all over her body, was also hospitalized for six weeks, and again it cost more than $1,000. But it was worth it just to see them get well again.

Those hospital bills are in addition to weekly expenses for shots and neuterings. For example, all my outside cats wear rabies collars, so that nobody can pick them up for not being inoculated. I run a tab at the vet's, and every now and again, I hand over my credit card and wipe away the whole debt. Except then I have to pay it off with interest to the bank. It doesn't ever seem to end, but I'm not complaining. Somehow I always find enough money to do whatever is necessary to keep all the cats well.

Cat food costs me between $15 and $20 a day, every day, three hundred and sixty-five days a year. I buy it wholesale from a large pet food warehouse, or it would cost a lot more. I like to give my cats variety. I feed them expensive foods like Iams, Whiskas, Fresh Catch, Sheba—I bribe the outside cats with luxury foods. I'm always afraid of their eating bad food from the garbage, or poisoned food left around the feeding sites, but my outside cats have developed such fine palates that they now turn up their noses at garbage.

When I take Ginny on our walks, I bring with me clean cat dishes and fresh, filtered water. Our local water's no good; it contains impurities, rust, and a lot of chlorine. I used to buy expensive bottled water, but then I learned that it comes from New Jersey, not from the mountain streams they show on the labels, so I bought a filter system. I used to use lightweight plastic dishes, the kind takeout Chinese food comes in, but they would blow away in the wind, so now I use heavy stoneware bowls and I wash them every day.

When we go on foot, Ginny and I, I start out by carrying around fifteen pounds of dry and canned food, water, and bowls. We have three routine feeding stops. Paradise, the tree on the strip of concrete near my home, and in good weather, Ramona's old feeding place on Miller Street. Sometimes I break up the routine by going back home to unload the empty pop-top cans, the empty water bottles, and the dirty dishes to be washed. Then we load up again and go out to finish the feedings.

During the ice storm when we found Rosie, Ramona fell and broke her hip. Her companion took care of all her one hundred and forty cats. She's recovering, but I've added some of her routes to mine, wherever I could reach on foot. The sites that can only be reached by car Sheilah has adopted. Ramona's neighbors circulated a petition to get rid of her, claiming that her house stunk, but I visited her and the house was spotless. It didn't smell at all. Another example of the meanness of people who don't like cats.

Miller Street used to be on my daily walking route, but it's a mile from my house, so in bad weather Sheilah feeds there morning and evening on her way to and from work. Miller Street includes gray-and-white and black-and-white cats, Klaatu, Gort, and one I call Saucer, because he's always waiting by the food dish. Now there are two other cats there, Silver Streak, a silver-striped tabby, and another black-and-white named Rufus. Sheilah often takes Miller Street and feeds any strays she meets as she drives, because the trunk of her Chevy Nova is always full of cat food. I always carry a few cans of food on me whenever I go out without Ginny, in case I meet somebody hungry on the way, which I almost always do.

NAMING MY CATS

I'm often asked how I come up with names for so many cats; where do these names come from? There's no special secret to naming a cat; most of my names come from my everyday surroundings. Good cat names can be found everywhere you look. For example, when Ginny found Vogue, Sheilah was with me and she was carrying a copy of *Vogue* fashion magazine. I saw the title and thought, That's a great name for this cat. Later, when Madonna came out with her "Vogue" single and video, I said to my cat, "Now you're a star."

Revlon was called Revlon because she was red, and she reminded me of makeup, particularly lipstick. Betty Boop was given her name when we took her home from the vet and I brought her down to Sheilah's apartment.

"What should we call her?" asked Sheilah, as we stared at the angry cat with no hind feet who had just joined the family. My eye fell on a little china figurine of Betty Boop that somebody had given Sheilah. And there was the name. Besides, when I was a kid I used to enjoy watching Betty Boop cartoons.

I've always loved reading ancient history and mythology, and that's where I got the names Thor, Clytemnestra, Venus, Penelope, Caesar, Calliope, Hector, and several others. Solomon and Sheba came from the Old Testament, of course, and Herod from the New Testament. Darlene was named after Roseanne's daughter on her television show, because the two of them are so much alike, independent and feisty. Klaatu came from a favorite old science-fiction movie, *The Day the Earth Stood Still*. The Chairman reminds me somehow of Frank Sinatra, don't ask me why. There are plenty of good cat names in the world; you don't have to call them all Kitty. Although Kitty is not such a bad name.

GINNY'S FRIENDS

I'm not the only person who loves Ginny. There's Penny, a neighbor who lives in the Parc Vendome apartment house and owns a number of cats; Penny feeds homeless cats on her terrace. We use the same veterinarian, and she has also placed cats for adoption with him and seen them go to loving homes. Many times she has helped Ginny in feeding, and she often phones me to tell me where she's seen an unfamiliar stray cat who needs our attention.

Ramona is a good friend, of course, and a loving heart. She has opened her home to one hundred forty cats and would love to have one hundred forty more. She appreciates everything that Ginny does to save them. She loves Ginny a lot. When I go to buy food from the wholesalers, I pick up cat food for Ramona, too. It makes her life a little easier.

I can't say enough in praise of my veterinarians, a man and a woman of kindness, compassion, and dedication. They really put the word *human* into "humane"; their gentle, expert care of the cats I've brought to them over the years, even the ones closest to death, has been nothing short of heroic. I've seen them pull far-gone animals back from the grave. Ginny and I could never have accomplished as much as we have if it weren't for Dr. Lewis Gelfand and Dr. Andrea Kuperschmid, staunch friends to Ginny and me and the cats. But Ginny's best friend and most enthusiastic supporter (after me, needless to say) is Sheilah Harris.

"I'm Ginny's mommy," she brags, and she's right. If it weren't for Sheilah, I never would have gone to our local animal shelter in the first place and found Ginny. Having seen her, I didn't want to take her out for a walk until Sheilah chimed in with her persuasions. She was Ginny's vocal champion from day one.

"Ginny got up and headed straight for Philip," says Sheilah. "She could hardly walk, yet she limped straight to him like a bee to a flower. She went from zero to nothing, that's the shape she was in, but she licked Philip's one good hand, and I could see that she'd made up her mind. She'd picked him out for her own. When we brought her home, she stayed curled up in Philip's arms all the way.

"I used to hate cats so much that even my best friend in the world had to lock hers up before I'd set foot in her house. But just knowing Ginny has turned my head around completely.

"I watched Ginny respond to cries for help," Sheilah explains, "and how injuries drew her to cats. Ginny understood their fear and would run and jump and strain to get near the cats, somehow finding them injured in their hiding places. Then she'd bark at me, which said to me plainly, 'Sheilah, do something!'

"I heard the sounds she made when she found that litter of week-old kittens, and watched her licking and grooming them just as a mother cat would. Philip put the kittens into his bathtub, which held them safe, and Ginny would stay in the tub with them, snuggling them, keeping them warm and sheltered by her body. I have to confess that I fell in love with those cute little kittens—me, the cat-hater!—and that started me on my love for cats.

"Ginny taught me about strays and rescuing and I saw how she felt about all living things. It was genuine emotion, and it convinced me that when an animal was hungry and in pain and needed help, we had to help. We had no choice. First, Ginny gave us no choice, and later, we made those rescue decisions on our own."

One of Sheilah's first enlightening experiences came when we were in her apartment one day, and Ginny started pulling towels out of the closet with her teeth, something she had never done before, while whimpering to get our attention.

"She wants to go out," I told Sheilah. "There's a cat in trouble out there somewhere."

We took her out, and that's when we found Venus, locked in a garage and emaciated almost to the point of death. That early adventure impressed Sheilah a lot, and she began to look at cats through new eyes.

"I could tell the cats were Ginny's family," she says, "when I saw how tender she was with Madame and Vogue and the others. But I'll always think of Ginny as part mine. I was with her from the very beginning. She has two homes, mine and Philip's, and she visits me every day to check up on my cats." Sheilah tells me that it's impossible not to want to be a part of Ginny's miracles.

"I never would have believed you if you told me this a

few years ago, but cats are my life now," Sheilah says, shaking her head, marveling. "That's why I don't speed on the parkway. I'm afraid of hitting a cat."

Sheilah is now known to the neighbors as the "Cat Lady." And some of our cats live down in Sheilah's apartment now, giving us all a little more room. Sheilah adores them; they are her family, and of course they get daily visits from Ginny, who romps with them and grooms them. She's part mother and part nurse for all the cats, Sheilah's and mine.

The ones I live with, my inside cats, number sixteen, but that's more than likely only a temporary number. I'm sure numbers seventeen and eighteen can't be far away. Then there are my terrace cats, who prefer not to live with us, but who come up to sleep and eat on my front terrace. The Chairman, Marble, Rembrandt, and Suzanne are some of those who prefer to use my place as a hotel rather than a home. In cold weather some of the outside cats like to cuddle and sleep together in the three carriers I keep on my terrace. We put food and fresh water out there every day.

Remember the first cat Ginny ever kissed on the nose? The one in the vacant lot that she met soon after she came to live with me? She was a lovely little kitten, a golden tabby with long hair. She was the very first homeless cat Ginny made me feed, Clytemnestra.

Maybe I should have taken Clytemnestra home with me. But I already had Ginny, and back then I didn't want a cat. It occurs to me now that if I'd taken her, perhaps I'd have kept the pussycat population down. I think she was the grandmother of many generations of long-haired cats, because many of the strays I feed are fluffy and some are golden.

As of this writing, we have found good homes for about sixty-five cats, and Sheilah and I have given our own homes to our sixteen inside cats. I'm proud of that record; I'm proud of myself and of Sheilah; I'm proudest of Ginny. Ginny loves all our cats, and they love her. They play together all the time, and she kisses them and they kiss her, but she is happiest, I think, when she's grooming one of the cats like its mother would. She loves to nibble their fur, and to lick them clean and smooth.

GINNY BECOMES FAMOUS

In 1993 I heard about a course given at the Learning Annex by Carol Wilbourn, a famous cat therapist. It was called "How to Talk to Your Cat." Because I was having some litter box problems with Betty Boop, who was occasionally using the sofa or the rug, I decided to take the class. At the end, Carol asked the audience, "How many cats do you have?" I raised my hand and said, "Eight." We talked for a little after the course was over, and I told her about Ginny and her remarkable way of saving homeless, starving, and especially, disabled cats. Carol said, "You ought to do a story."

Five days later, I got a phone call from the Learning Annex, telling me that the magazine *Good Housekeeping* wanted to get in touch with me. Should they give them my phone number? I said sure. And so, on the hottest day of the year, *Good Housekeeping* editor Phyllis Levy, a genuine cat-lover, came to see me with a magazine photographer and the writer Micki Siegel. I took them down to Sheilah's apartment to see the cats. But not one set of paws or whiskers was in sight. No cats anywhere.

Everybody looked at me dubiously, as though I were some nut wasting their time. "Are you sure there are cats here?"

I went back across the courtyard and got Ginny. When Ginny set her paw into Sheilah's apartment, the cats suddenly appeared like magic. Madame was the first one to come out, and she broke the ice. Then little Caesar appeared, followed by the others. They came out of every nook and cranny, and gathered around their Ginny. The photographer snapped a lot of pictures. At first, Ginny barked at the photographer; he turned out to be a smoker, and she hates the smell of cigarettes. After a while they left, and Ginny felt bad. She's a born ham, she loves being the center of attention, and she'd been getting a lot of it from the magazine people.

After Micki Siegel's article in *Good Housekeeping* came out, in June 1994, Ginny became something of a local celebrity. Many neighborhood people said, "I saw your dog in the magazine article." Some even offered me money for cat food, but I never accepted it. This is something I'd rather do on my own.

Of course, not everybody was so friendly. What I heard over and over was the question "What kind of life is that?"

"It's my life," I would answer. "And I'm happy with it."

Others were indignant that I would take cats to the vet for neutering. "Neutering animals is against the will of God," they would shout at me.

But I don't think it's God's will that so many unwanted animals are brought into the world to live short, difficult lives and perish miserably. I think it's infinitely better to make pets of the animals already here, to bring them into the warm, and love them.

Another thing people ask me is, "Have you ever thought of getting another dog?" Well, once I did. When Ginny and I paid our visit to the shelter, I saw a dog in a cage who appealed to me. At that time, my only cats were Vogue and Madame, so I gave a moment's thought to bringing this dog home as another companion for Ginny.

But Kenny, the shelter worker, shook his head. "No," he warned me, "this dog kills cats."

And that was the end of my taking *that* dog. After that, thanks to Ginny, the cats came so thick and fast there was never any more thought of a second dog.

Ginny once bumped into one of her puppies at the animal shelter. He was named Paddy, and he was fully grown. Man, was he grown! He was at least twice Ginny's size, and had a beautiful shiny black coat. He didn't recognize Ginny as his mother, and was eager to get at her and make mincemeat out of her. Also, he hated cats!

Paddy had been adopted as a puppy, but he had grown to a size and heft that his owners couldn't handle, so they brought him back to the shelter and put him up for adoption again. His story had a happy ending. Paddy went to a home that had three growing boys in the family, and they were thrilled to have a large, energetic pup to play with. Paddy became very protective of them, and made a wonderful family pet and watchdog. He's still with them.

GINNY'S ENEMIES

It's hard to accept, but not everybody on Long Island loves my Ginny as Sheilah Harris and I do. She has enemies, people who are ignorant about cats, hate and fear them, and don't want to see them saved from death and fed every day. There's one guy I think of as "the Neighborhood Poisoner," and I'm sure in my mind that he's responsible for the sudden disappearance of a number of my outside cats. If I could catch him at it, I'd fix him for good. I'm not talking violence, I'm talking a report to the Long Island Humane Society and fines and maybe even some jail time. But so far I have no real proof, although we did have one memorable face-off in which he revealed himself.

"What are you doing?" he asked me one day when he saw me at the tree.

"I'm feeding these cats." He could see this plainly; he wasn't blind.

"Well, you better stop it."

"Why? What did these cats ever do to you?"

He stuck his lower lip out and glared at me. "They don't belong around here, and they carry diseases. I'm gonna poison them."

"You do, and I'll come after you so hard your whole family will yell 'Ow!'"

Even if he did poison some of my outside cats, I'm sure he wasn't the only one. A lot of people in my neighborhood are not happy about cats being fed near them. They don't like to see them congregating, and most of all they don't like to hear them. Mating cats do make a lot of noise, especially when people are trying to sleep. But when I gather them up and have them neutered, they don't mate anymore, and are much more quiet at night, so they really ought to welcome Ginny's and my efforts. Of course, being human, they don't.

ANGEL GINNY

Over the years, as Ginny's fame has grown, a lot of people have asked me, "Do you think Ginny is an angel?"

I've thought long and hard about my dog Ginny's unique gift for seeking out, finding, and rescuing sick, injured, and disabled cats. I believe that Ginny must have known that Madame was stone deaf as soon as she laid eyes on her. I believe that she understood completely that the kitten Jackie was totally blind, that Revlon was half-blind, that Topsy would never walk, that Betty Boop had no hind feet, and that I myself had only one good arm. I believe as I believe the sun will rise in the east tomorrow that Ginny must have been sent by God to do the work she does.

Otherwise, how could she have persuaded a cat-hater like Sheilah Harris to turn into a cat-lover with a houseful of cats and kittens?

Ginny is still a magnet for disabilities, animal and human. For two years she had a Labrador friend, a beautiful dark dog named Coffee. We met Coffee almost every day on our walks. He was always carrying a stick in his mouth. The first time she saw him, Ginny ran toward him.

"Hold on to her!" his owner yelled to me. "Don't let your

dog get near mine. He doesn't like other dogs, and he'll attack her if she touches his stick."

But it was already too late. Ginny was nose to nose with Coffee. Immediately, he dropped the stick on the ground, and allowed Ginny to pick it up in her own mouth. He didn't even growl.

The stick was very important to Coffee because he was completely blind. There must have been some sense of security in that piece of wood he always carried around with him. Nobody could get his stick away from him except his beloved owner and my Ginny. As soon as she saw him, she would run over to him and bite down on that stick, and he would allow her to take it out of his mouth. They did that almost every day for about two years, until Coffee and his owner moved to Florida.

And here's another instance of Ginny's special radar for disabilities. Not long ago when I was riding on the train from the city, Sheilah came to the station to meet me and brought Ginny with her. A man was waiting there at a bus stop. As soon as Ginny saw him, she wanted to get close to him, and she started to pull on her leash. She whimpered and barked. Although he didn't appear to be, the man was blind. Sheilah didn't know it until he took his folding white cane from his pocket. She let Ginny go to the man. He bent down and petted Ginny, and she stayed by him for more than twenty minutes, until his bus came. Sheilah could hardly wait to tell me about it when my train pulled in. One more example of how Ginny responds to people with disabilities.

Somebody asked me if I believe in angels. Even if I didn't

believe in them at one time, I do now. I really do believe that Ginny is an angel, sent down to do this specific rescue work. When you consider how many lives she has saved and made better—starting with my own—you can see that she's got to be on a mission from heaven.

Ginny and I have been together five years now. We share a birthday, April 1. She's now six years old. We made a pact, the two of us, when I brought her home from the shelter. I promised that I would love her, and keep her, and treat her as a member of my family. She promised me that she would live a very long life, and stay with me a very long time, and I intend to see she keeps that promise.

What of the future? I hope and pray that it's more of the present, that we can go on with our work, Ginny and I, for many years to come. If I could have my dream come true, I'd have a large place with lots of land. I'd have hundreds of cats, hundreds of dogs, and General Ginny would be in charge of everything. That would make me very happy. That would make Ginny very happy.

My dog, Ginny, saved my life. She found me depressed, unhappy, and insecure about my future. All by herself, Ginny set my feet upon a new path. At first, I was somewhat reluctant to go down that path, but she and the cats won me over completely. Thanks entirely to her efforts, I have a busy, active, happy, and useful life.

What is an angel? Most people believe that they are invisible beings with celestial powers granted by God. They are all around us. An angel watches over mortals in their everyday lives, looks after them and guides them through life, intervening at the right moment to save them from death and disaster. Well, how is that any different from who Ginny is and what she does? And where is it written that an angel must have wings and not a wagging tail? I believe completely that God sent Ginny down to earth to rescue cats who would have died without her intervention. I believe that God sent Ginny down to rescue me. Without her intervention I would have remained a bitter, useless man.

Now, every day for me is meaningful, as an animal rescue worker, freelance, self-employed, and unpaid. I am needed, as I was never before needed in my life, by all the homeless and hungry mistreated animals. In my old life, I had plenty of fun, but no real happiness. Now I know the true happiness of living for others, and the true happiness of being surrounded by creatures I love. Ginny and the cats are my family, and we love being together.

Most of all, little Ginny—part schnauzer, part Siberian husky, part angel from heaven—has taught me the most important lesson in life, that life is not worth living without love, that giving love is more rewarding than getting it, and that the humblest creatures, the least advantaged creatures, are worthy of the greatest outpouring of love. It's a spiritual message, that all life is precious, all life is short, and that, just as human beings have immortal souls, so do animals have immortal souls, because they, too, were created by God.

If that's not heaven's message, I'd like to know what is.